The Times Book of Prayers

The Times Book of Prayers

Edited by
Ruth Gledhill

Illustrations by the Pupils of
Rugby School

Mowbray

Mowbray
A Cassell imprint

Wellington House
125 Strand
London
WC2R 0BB

PO Box 605
Herndon
VA 20172

First published 1997
Reprinted 1998

For the 1998 reprint, corrections have been made to the
following prayers: no. 63 (page 28), no. 101 (page 46), no. 195
(page 91) and no. 232 (page 111), and no. 188, *Morning prayer*,
has now been printed in its entirety on page 140.

British Library Cataloguing-in-Publication Data
A catalogue record for this book is available from the British
Library.

ISBN 0-264-67442-1

Typeset by Pantek Arts, Maidstone, Kent
Printed and bound in Great Britain by
Biddles Ltd, Guildford and King's Lynn

Contents

Acknowledgements

My special thanks to Leonard Latiff, Esther Foreman, Rachel
Thackeray, Jenni Dandrea, Eleanor Salmond and Laura Benjamin,
all students on work experience at *The Times*, who were the
answers to my prayers for help in editing this book. My thanks to
the Bishop of London, the Right Revd Richard Chartres, for
sending me Anthony de Mello's *Sadhana, A Way to God*, after I
confessed to feeling useless at praying. My thanks also to my
husband Andrew, whose prayers that it might soon be ended and
that I would be back to normal are answered by this book's
publication. My thanks to my editor Peter Stothard and news
editor Graham Duffill, for their forbearance when concentration
on this project at times affected my concentration on my daily
work of reporting religion for *The Times*. Thanks to Ian Burke and
the pupils of Rugby School for supplying the illustrations. And
finally, thanks be to God that it is completed.

To Rachel

Introduction

The invitation by *The Times* to readers to send in prayers they had composed for possible publication in a book grew out of our growing conviction that, in spite of a continuing decline in church-going, interest in and belief in religion and God remain steadfast. We felt there were many thousands out there who had a real and active spiritual life, and that some small proportion of these might feel moved to put pen to paper in prayer. We were overwhelmed by the response. Dozens of prayers, each with its own intensely personal story to tell, arrived on my desk daily for many months. I was at once staggered and humbled, and felt wholly inadequate to the task of selecting the inevitably small proportion that could be included in this book.

Cardinal Hume, addressing the headmasters of Catholic public schools recently, said: 'Teaching the young how to pray and not simply requiring them to pray at set times and on certain occasions is both profoundly educational and spiritually invigorating.' With the decline of institutional religion, personal prayer is becoming more important in the lives of individuals. For those who believe, as I do, that human existence comprises three essential components – the physical, the mental and the spiritual – prayer is as essential a part of daily life as food and love. But just as children need to be taught how to eat properly and how to love, so they need to be taught how to pray. The instinctive reaching out to God might be natural, as the centuries of religious history suggest, as is the instinctive yearning to love. The ability to pray effectively must be taught.

Prayer need not be merely a means of personal expression, or a communication with God, or a Higher Power, as some of these contributors have referred to their concept of a supreme being. It can be a tool towards achieving other ends. According to Billy Graham, the three elements of successful evangelism are 'Prayer, prayer and prayer'. People who pray regularly are often calmer and more relaxed, making them agents of peace in highly stressed workplaces. In government, the MPs with highly developed prayer lives are often those who are most effective in building unity and avoiding conflict within their parties. Prayer is a means of focusing on the present, of letting go and handing over to God, trusting He will take care of the result.

One of the most helpful books on prayer is the best-selling *Sadhana, A Way to God*, by Anthony de Mello (Doubleday, £6.95). 'Most priests and religious equate prayer with thinking. That is their downfall,' he says. He cites a Hindu guru who told a Jesuit seeking advice to concentrate on his breathing. 'The air you breathe is God. You are breathing God in and out. Be aware of that, and stay with that awareness,' the guru said. Through prayer and meditation, he writes, it is possible to attain things that money cannot buy, such as wisdom, serenity, joy and God. Too many people live in the past, regretting mistakes, feeling guilty about sins committed, gloating over former achievements, resenting injuries caused by other people. Or they live in the future, dreading calamities, unpleasantness, anticipating future joys, dreaming of future events. 'To succeed in prayer it is essential to develop the instinct to make contact with the present and to stay there,' he writes.

The prayers in this book are, to me, examples of what Sadhana believes: that prayer can be a place where contemplation is born, and prayer becomes a transforming power and source of never-ending peace. Many of these contributors wrote in response to the August edition of the magazine of the Fellowship of Christian Writers, which referred to our request for prayers. Others heard from friends or acquaintances. Some included in their letters extra prayers that their prayers be accepted. Some were prayers written many years ago, and which had proved effective in the authors' life but had never had a wider use. Others were written in response to our invitation.

Some prayers were excellent and helpful, but could not be included in the book because of their length or format. One example was 'Pray your Way around your Home', by Brian Anker of Cambridge, a format for meditating and giving thanks throughout the house, including the kitchen, dining-room, bathroom and bedroom. Another, submitted by Joe McKenzie of Newcastle upon Tyne, was an inspiring meditation for the week following Easter Day. 'Touch us, O Lord, and let us hold your hands as we say My Lord and My God,' he wrote for the Saturday after Easter.

David Wright, of Norwich, referred me to the hymn by James Montgomery (1771–1854), a newspaper editor imprisoned twice for his radical views:

O Thou by whom we come to God,
    The Life, the Truth, the Way,

The path of prayer Thyself hast trod:
    Lord, teach us how to pray.

Prayer is the soul's sincere desire,
   Uttered or unexpressed;

The motion of a hidden fire
   That trembles in the breast.

Chris Willis, of Hertfordshire, offered an extract from the story
Ludmilla, by Paul Gallico. A prayer can be a cry in the darkness for
help when all seems lost, he writes, 'a song, a poem, a kind deed,
a reaching for beauty, or the strong quiet inner affirmation of
faith'. He continues: 'A prayer in fact can be anything that is
created of God that turns to God.'

Some of the most moving contributions included a prayer that
a son might live, written by a casualty officer after her son
sustained serious head injuries in an accident, so serious he was
not expected to survive. His mother says: 'All the best medical
treatment was available but the prayers of our many friends and
relatives were the "extra ingredient" that helped him to recovery
– not yet back to full health but doing remarkably well.' Others
suggest that prayers can be written to their own special formulas,
with resonances of ancient prayers like that of St Francis of
Assissi. One prayer was written after the author lost her daughter
because of a fatal genetic abnormality. She says: 'It isn't perhaps a
usual topic for a prayer but to lose a child before birth in
circumstances where a pre-natal diagnosis has been made is
surely a modern-day situation which causes great sorrow and
pain that is often unrecognized by more traditional prayers of
mourning for a loved one.'

The shortest prayers were: 'Dear Father God – Help,' submitted
by Roger Lunch of Romford, Essex, and 'Lord, give me a job
today.' The author of the latter admits this is 'not the sort of
prayer one ought to pray' but reports that God set His price.
Within an hour of praying this prayer, the phone rang with a job
offer. His new employer, an agnostic, persuaded him to seek
ordination, and he was ordained priest in 1967. 'Clearly it is the
kind of spontaneous request which God answered, for my
immediate need – but for his long-term purpose,' he writes.

Many prayers clearly emerged from deep suffering, and
because of this most came from older or retired people, although
children were also represented. Some of these had also clearly
experienced difficulties in their brief lives. Some revealed a
desperate search for a contact with God that churches seem not to
be fulfilling.

Some prayers emerged from unbelievably tragic stories of loss. There was the prayer written by a parent after his son died in a car crash while on holiday in Mallorca, a prayer he cannot recall writing, and which appears to be the voice of the boy speaking to his mother. Others show deep faith. The writer of *Find me, O Lord*, a 67-year-old widow, says: 'I did not know the Lord until He called me at the age of 64. I was baptized one week after my 65th birthday, on Pentecost Day. I was given this gift of *prayer, poems and prophecy*. I cannot speak prayers, but am given them from the Lord as I pray to Him. As I was a backward child it is even more amazing to me. This is the only way I can pass on the love of Jesus. I give them to those people who need them, those who are in grief, pain, sadness, and to those who do not know what love, joy and peace is, in Jesus. This I did not know myself until old age. Thank you for this chance, maybe, to spread the word of God to many more people.'

Many contributors sent in prayers they had written in response to a request or a need. One example was the Revd Vincent Markland, who retired early from full-time ministry in July 1995 and became temporary Anglican chaplain to the Royal Manchester Children's Hospital. 'I commenced this ministry in April last year and very soon discovered that many parents require help in praying for their sick children,' he says. 'They want to pray but don't know what to say.' He leaves copies of his prayer on the hospital's information desk. More than 20 copies are taken each week, and it was even translated into Italian for the parents of a child from Florence.

The Revd Simon Baynes's prayer for writers is one I personally shall turn to regularly.

And there cannot be many people who have not hoped desperately for some sign that God is listening at all, as expressed eloquently by Frank Keetley to 'God's answering machine'. But my favourite prayer of all is the *Prayer for Arnaud de Contades*, by Canon Ian Dunlop, former chancellor of Salisbury Cathedral. Both poetic and spiritual, he makes with greater style and elegance the most effective prayer that I know, and one I say each day without fail: 'Thy will, not mine, be done.' This was a prayer that came truly both from the heart and from the head.

Ruth Gledhill
June 1997

1

O Lord, take the 'I' out of me
Serving others as for Thee
Give me strength to do my best
Cheerfully and full of zest
And gratitude for being fit
In evenings thankfulness to sit
In visionary terms at Thy feet
From earthly worries to retreat
Into holiness and peace
until the time of my release
Then on heavenly wings to soar
Into Thy presence evermore.

Barbara Hodder, *81, of Abbeydale, Gloucester.*

2

I thank the plains
  for without them there could be no mountains.

I thank the shadows
  for they have made me feel the warmth of sunlight.

I thank want
  for it has taught me how to share abundance.

I thank my enemies
  for forcing me to grow in strength
  and learn compassion.

I thank fear
  for without it courage would mean nothing.

I thank the moments of grief and loss
  for they have made me learn to cherish joy.

I thank the Universe.

All passes
I bless it in its passing.

All endures
I bless it in its oneness.

Susan Castillo, *a lecturer in English literature at Glasgow University.*

3 A golfer's grace

For drives that soar
For chips that hold;
For putts that drop
When twice too bold;
For food and friends
On golfing days;
To God we give
Our thanks and praise.

Very Revd Alan Warren, *a retired provost, of Hunstanton, Norfolk.*

Oscar Viney, aged 15

4 A carer's prayer

Lord, it is four years since his father died
There are only two of us now
Lord in your mercy, help me.
Give me strength to care for my son
At night when he is not well
Lord in your mercy, help me.
Give me health in mind and body
To cope from day to day
Let not the path be too hard
Lord in your mercy, help me. Amen.

Joan Pritchard, *of Tredegar, Gwent.*

5 Cuddle down

*The author composed this cradle song for her son Fala, now aged four,
when he was a baby. It is sung to Brahms Lullaby.*

Cuddle down, little Fala,
Underneath your wee duvet,
Jesus bless you
Keep you safe
And guard you through the night.
You have lots of happy memories
Of a day full of fun,
Snuggle down now,
Dream sweetly
And tomorrow will come.

Mrs Romy Newell, *of Longformacus, Duns, Berwickshire.*

Derek Wing Hang Ho, aged 15

6

Dear God, help us to see
That prayer without purpose
Is as empty
As purpose without prayer. Amen.

Mrs Gloria Metcalfe, *a retired nursery nurse, of Ramsbottom, Lancashire.*

7

Lord,
Rule my heart,
Rein my tongue. Amen.

Donald Butcher, *a retired solicitor, of Grantham, Lincolnshire.*

8

It worries me to think that sometimes, Lord,
I catch myself wishing my life away.
When I'm queuing in a shop or waiting to get somewhere
I say to myself, 'Come on, come on,
I wish I was there, I wish it was done.'
I just haven't come to terms with being patient, you see.

But there are times when I think it is good
To be impatient for a change.
Not so much wanting to take steps into the future to shorten a
    lifetime,
More as skipping forward to the next bit of activity,
Where I can become involved, participate, be fulfilled.

Patience is a virtue, they say, Lord.
But I am impatient to do my share
To right some wrongs and lend a hand
And strike a blow for the power of good
On a planet turned old before its time
By the heavy hand of handy Man.
So if sometimes I lose my cool
And find some waiting endless,

Channel my thoughts towards my next goal
So that when the chance comes to do my bit
I won't need to build myself up
Or doubt my ability to succeed,
I'll just do it, in Your Name
As best I know how.

And if I don't have time to say thanks just then
When there's so much going on,
And I'm in the thick of the action,
Seizing my opportunity;
I'll say thank you now, in anticipation
Of Your helping hand when I need it. Amen.

David Farebrother, *teacher, of Banbury, Oxfordshire.*

9 An evening prayer in York Minster

Here, where the silence presses on my ears, in the darkening
    shadows of the nave,
I kneel, alone, in silent prayer.
Above me the soaring stone fades into dusk and the windows ebb
    into darkness,
Their colours melting into an overall grey.
In the silence the walls sing with praises long past, and the silent
    footsteps
Of a myriad worshippers resound throughout.
Unseen, unheard, unfelt, I am embraced with love and comfort.
Here, in the dusk, alone, I am in a multitude.
Here, in the cold, unheated space, I am warmed by the rich patina
    of love and charity,
Which seeps from every cranny of the walls. Here, countless
    hearts have worshipped,
And left within these walls a love of God and man, which is passed
From heart to heart to comfort and heal.
Thank you, Lord, for this moment of understanding,
Which carries me forward, in confidence, through
The tumult and turmoil of my world.

Bill Goulding, *of Nelson, Lancashire.*

10 A doubter's prayer

Forgive me, Lord
(If Lord there be)
When I deny thee.

For I, in doubt,
Would (cowardly),
Still crucify
Thee.

But grant me grace, O Lord,
To see
Thy presence nigh me.

That I may live,
From doubt set free,
To glorify Thee.

Margaret King, *of Lymm, Cheshire.*

11 An insomniac's prayer

Each line of this prayer should be said with eyes shut, breathing regularly and saying each line while inhaling.

Dear God
Help me
End this
Despair.
Give me
Quiet hope
To shed
Nightmare.
I've tried
To last
Out this
Long day.
Show me
How to
Find the
Right way.
Now please
Grant me
From pain
Sweet sleep,
And send
Me to
Dreamless
Rest deep. Amen.

Katherine Polland, aged 15

Mrs Maureen McKee, *a retired teacher, of Doonbank, Ayr.*

12

Lord, give me patience when my temper frays,
Lord, give me humour on the bluesy days.
Give me humility when things go well,
Teach me to listen more than tell.

Lord, lift my spirits when things look black,
Lord, keep me forward looking, never back.
Keep me from anger when things go wrong,
Make me contented where I belong. Amen.

Gay Headley, *a care assistant, of Llanferres, Denbighshire.*

13 The simple art

Sometimes I wonder, Lord, just what you plan
For me. It isn't power, or great success,
Or tranquil and domestic happiness
That flows from motherhood; and though I can
Do several things a little better than
One might expect, I really must confess
To no outstanding gift. Yet, none the less,
I have a sense that since my life began
It has been planned by you. What might appear
An accident, or Fate's perversity,
Is seen, when my objections disappear,
To be your act of generosity.
I wonder, Lord, perhaps you put me here
To learn the simple art of being me.

Mary Spain, *a writer and teacher, of west London.*

14

Dear God,
Nothing I can ever do will make me truly worthy of
    this precious loan of life you've made to me.
Every day I am tempted to follow my own selfish way.
Please show me ever more clearly Your will
    and teach me how to put it into practice with all my heart.
Reminded that even Jesus, so perfect in your Love, sought to do
    Your will and not his own.

Sarayen Day, *of Newport, Shropshire.*

15 Who You are

I pray
That mankind
Agrees
On one,
Universal,
Rational
Definition
  of
Who You are.

Kyvelie Papas MD, *of west London.*

Esosa Egonmwan, aged 15

16

Thank you for the worm and slug,
    the way the worm wriggles and makes holes in my Nanna's
    lawn,
    the way the slug nibbles through my grandfather's beans.
Thank you for the caterpillar,
    the way he turns from a green-fingered gardener's pest to
    beautiful butterfly.
I like the little worms and slugs and every little bug. Amen.

Tennille Rees, *aged 9, of Oakleigh House School, Swansea.*

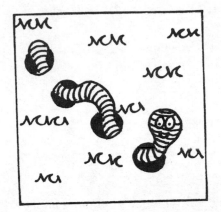

Katherine Polland, aged 15

17

Thank you, Lord,
 for being my anchor in times of storm,
 for being my light in times of darkness,
 for being my friend in times of isolation,
 for being my rock in times of doubt,
 for being my saviour,
 for being my God.
Thank you, Lord, for the joy of knowing you.

Yvonne Portch, *of Addington, Surrey.*

18 On the loss of a loved one

I will not believe you are gone from me
Although you are not here. I cannot see
Your familiar shape, or feel your touch,
Nor hear your voice... It hurts so much...
I long to have you back with me,
A way of life that used to be.
The inward turmoil will not cease,
I cannot find an inner peace.
A world so strange, yet nothing new.
I am alone. I have not you.

Edwina Bedeman, *of Bridgwater, Somerset.*

19 When faced with a challenge

Dear Lord,
Please give me the Wisdom
   the Energy
   the Time
 to do this job properly.

Christopher Compston, *a circuit judge*, *of west London.*

20

Merciful Father,

You know that depression plunges us into the slough of despond, where all self-respect is lost.

Dear Lord, who forgives us everything, teach us to forgive ourselves. Help us to understand that we too can be an instrument in the fulfilment of others.

Maureen Clarke, *of Coopersale, Epping, Essex.*

21 A prayer on forgiveness

Foolish words often spoken
Our hearts we bring to you
Regretting things not said or done
Grant us peace O Lord
Indifference to the needs of others
Violence, rage and anger
Envelop us with your love
Never let go.
Empty lives and fruitless goals
Shameless sin
Save us Lord and forgive us.

Anne Perkin, *schoolteacher, of Kidderminster, Worcestershire.*

22 To my guardian angel

O Seraph that doth guard this ill-used life,
O thee that rescues me from sinful strife,
I am unworthy of thy watchful love,
Let alone that of my Lord above.
Alone, a path I blindly seek;
Against temptation I am weak.
Of this sad fact I am all too aware,

And yet I long to be a fitting object of thy care:
I can but pray that, one glad day, thy love for me
Will be one half as just as mine for thee.

John Grealish, *aged 13, of Kensington, London.*

23 A prayer for those whose hearts conceal pain they cannot
voice – through guilt, through shame, through
embarrassment, through grief, through fear; those who bear
their own condemnation and dare not ask for comfort.

The driver who has killed or maimed;
The mother who has reared an unworthy child;
The man or woman who should condemn a brother or sister;
The parent who through a lapse in vigilance has seen a child hurt;
The workman whose imperfect work has had tragic consequences;
The 'other woman' who must stifle her love;
The illicit lover, mute and tempted;
The bereaved who understand too late;
Those who have voiced their hate but not their love;
All who are living with irrevocable acts and words.

Dear God, banish us not entirely,
    but grant that, surpassing all understanding,
Thy Holy Spirit may come to us,
    to heal and rekindle.

Margaret Crofts, *of Cromford, Derbyshire.*

24 A prayer for service

Lord, I am a tool in your hands;
Take me and use me
As you will,
When you will,
If you will.
But grant this only,
That my edge
May be sharp,
And bright,
And clean,
And ready for service. Amen.

Revd Thomas Desert, *of Bedford.*

25

This prayer and prayers 26–28 were submitted by Hilary Jakeman after she asked her young people's group, aged 10 to 14, to write prayers.

Dear Lord,
Please help people to be good and kind in their work and in their
    play,
Never to be greedy, or spiteful to others, and never to steal.
And please make the people who haven't got friends make new
    friends,
because a friend is someone who walks in when everyone else
    walks out. Amen.

Zoe-Anne Al-Tahiri, *aged 12, of Harrow, Middlesex.*

26

Pray for all the people who have no family, or anyone who has no
    one to turn to. Let them talk to people.
Pray for all the people who are ill. Pray for them to get better.

Heather Turner, *aged 11, of Harrow, Middlesex.*

27

Pray for all those people who are dying right
now, and that football goes well next season
and in Euro '96, for the people that work on
boats, taxis, planes, trains and buses to keep
them tidy and safe for us.

Denis O'Neill, *aged 12, of Harrow, Middlesex.*

Edward Ellis, aged 15

28

Dear Lord,
Please help all those who are in any way suffering, especially my
nan who is suffering a lot in hospital, also for everyone else who
is in pain or has recently been bereaved. Amen.

Laura Turner, *aged 14, of Harrow, Middlesex.*

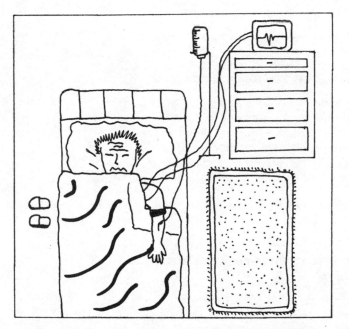

Jimmy Hung Hing Leung, aged 15

29

*This prayer has been adapted from a prayer of the Church of South
India.*

Be present, be present O Jesus
As you were in the midst of your disciples
And be made known to us in the breaking of the bread
The bread of your sacrament, the bread of your word
And the bread of our daily life together.

Dame Cicely Saunders, *chairman, St Christopher's Hospice, London.*

30 I implore You, Lord

Dear Lord,
I implore you to ask your Father to let peace come to our country.
We, the people of Ireland, do want peace, not war. Politicians
from all over the world have tried to end this bitter war, and have
failed bitterly. How many more people have to suffer, to be killed,
leaving mothers with young children to bring up?
I love you more than anything on this earth, just say the word and
I will follow your command. Amen.

Maureen Connolly, *of Sion Mills, Co. Tyrone.*

31 A prayer for prayers

O Ascended Lord Jesus, take my poor prayers
into thine own, correcting them, and
supplying them with what they lack; and
present them, O crucified One, at the
throne of the Father, for the blessing of
myself and those for whom I have prayed. Amen.

Revd Robert Faulkner, *a retired Anglican clergyman, of Woodstock, Oxfordshire.*

32 Prayer before worship

My Lord and my God,
I bow in prayer in your Presence.
Help my mind and spirit to worship you in this hour,
Inspire and strengthen the one who leads our worship,
Give your peace and blessing to those who cannot be here,
Bless all who share in our worship now.
I offer my prayer and praise in the Name of Jesus Christ. Amen.

Revd Neil Graham, *a Methodist minister, of Thirsk, Yorkshire.*

33 Fountain of grace

Cleanse me afresh in my hour
of need; where beats a heart

by nature rebellious, cause
its pulse to cease from sin.

Immerse me fully in thy fountain
of grace, draw near that I may
know the prompting of thy Spirit's will.

All my unrighteousness lay bare
before me and guide this helpless
soul to place the remainder of
his life upon the altar of repentance.

James Sherman, *industrial engineer, of Bangor, Co. Down.*

34 Lord, I am tired

Lord, I am tired, so tired! I have had a busy time, and the older I
become, the more tired I am. Sometimes I am even too tired to
think straight. Not only can't I remember things and people and
places, but sometimes I even forget what I started to say. And,
when it comes to prayer, my Lord, I so often forget what I want to
pray about, and certainly I do not pray as I ought.
So, good and dear Lord, I bring my tired self to you, for you
know me better than I know myself. I come not seeking some
magic cure for my tiredness, but asking that you will accept me as
I am – forgive me, help me, hold me and grant me of your peace.
Here I am Lord, come now to me, for your name's sake. Amen.

Revd Peter Mark, *a retired URC minister and former headmaster, of
Penarth, Wales.*

35 Prayer for a teenage daughter

I was young once –
Remind me, Lord.

I was in love – many times,
Remind me, Lord.

I was rude – sometimes impossible,
Remind me, Lord.

For I was loved, unconditionally,
As I will love this daughter, too.
On anxious days, on happy days,
Thanking you Lord, for all her growing-up days.

Eileen Balmforth, *of Yorkley, Gloucestershire.*

36

O Lord who speaks to us in the quiet of the hills, in the mystery of the forests, by the sea and in the mountains, speak also in that still, small voice within our souls. Amen.

Canon Charles Johnson, *a canon of Chichester Cathedral and Provost of Seaford College, of Petworth, West Sussex.*

37 Submission

In whomsoever's mind I am remembered,
In whomsoever's heart I yet may dwell,
Take my name, erase, replace it
With Thine Own, Emmanuel.

Peter Harris, *of Burford, Oxford.*

38 Serving the needs of others

Lord, when I am tempted to make myself indispensable, grant me the grace and common sense to make myself redundant.

Phil Boorman, *consultant in mathematics education, Yorkley, Gloucestershire.*

39 Prayer song

A spider's web mimics the sun,
A fish swallows the sea,
A child counts to a hundred-and-one,
And I call out to Thee.
If You can hear the grass emerge,
The soft pulse of the sea,
If You can hear the widow's dirge,
Then there is hope for me.
Hear my ragged voice, O Lord,
As I call out to Thee.
Teach me with Your Holy Word,
And I'll call out to Thee.

John Sexton, *of Kenmare, Co. Kerry, Ireland.*

40

If, when the light shades close in, lengthen,
Change as if to dusk,
Then may I see Thy holy face, as one,
Joined on a beam of light.
The portals of this world closed, only a sudden beam
That fills our dreams, makes holiness mine.
In such places will Thy shroud of endless divinity
Take hold, make 'Thy will be done' as one,
An endless prayer for all those still to climb
Your mountain of life's goodness, kindness, knowing
No fashionable trend.
Only Thy endless peace, no more changing-of-being;
Thy will be done my song, my hope,
My very joyous dream to lend time still here
Its glow, its only way to end. Amen.

Pamela Ames-McGrath, *of Bath.*

41 A prayer of petition

Father grant to me, through your Holy Spirit,
The patience of Job,
The wisdom of Solomon,
The faith of Abraham,
The obedience of Moses,
The courage of Elijah,
The constancy of Jeremiah,
The repentance of St Peter,
The hope of St Paul,
And, above all, the Love of Jesus.
Now and forever.

Rodney Pope, *of Langport, Somerset.*

42

We break no bonds nor bridge
        steel barriers
When we meet, for we are not
        'I' and 'It',
But 'Thou and Thou', O 'Thou
        and Thou', again.

Dorothy Ann McGregor, *of Accrington, Lancashire.*

43

Lord, flow through me,
Use me as the channel
    through which Your Holy Spirit can work.
But Lord, I know that there are some things in my life
    which cause a blockage.
There's debris from past hurts and slights
    that seems to have sunk down out of sight –
But I am conscious that the silt can still muddy the waters.
Then there are the small pebbles I have kept –
Reminders of pain endured; the fears and the anxieties
    of what might have been and still might yet come.
Lord, help me to clear away the rubbish
So that the Water of Life may flow freely.
And what's this, Lord – weeds?
Where have they sprung from?
Where is the root – ah, now I see!
The old habits, the sins you forgave
But which I didn't fully yield.
The root was left behind when they were cut away
And insidiously they have grown in secret.
Why, there's envy and resentment and bitterness!
I was so sure I had dealt with them.
You mean I can *never* stop weeding, Lord,
Or clearing away the debris?
Forgive me, Lord, and give to me a pure and upright heart in
    your sight so that nothing – absolutely nothing – can stand in
    the way of being a channel for your love. Amen.

Revd Mary Tweed, *of Herne Bay, Kent.*

44

God our Father,
Jesus our Saviour,
Holy Spirit our Comforter,
Blessed Trinity.
        In your mercy and love hear this prayer, this earnest plea for
a quiet mind. Take away the jangled, muddled, wretched, wrong
thoughts which screech and clamour. O hush their noise and fury
with the blessings of your quietness, stillness and calm. Bring
silence and come in the silence.

As with all our hearts we truly seek you, may we find you; for in you alone is our peace, and to you alone is all honour, praise and glory, now and forever. Amen.

Dorothy Dudley, *of Pickering, North Yorkshire.*

45 Night prayer

Lord, while I offer silent prayers to You,
May I drift to peaceful sleep,
And as I sleep, may I dream
That all my prayers come true;
Until the dawn, when sleep has gone,
Then may Your peace remain
The whole day through. Amen.

Julie Holness, *of Tankerton, Whitstable, Kent.*

46 Is it b or d?

Written worbs
Are a mystery
I struggle
to becipher.
They say
I'm byslexic
And mubble up
My b's and d's.
Dut I besire
Help!
So please Gob,
Unravel
My drain.
Stop things
Deing dack
To front.

Muriel Simpson, *of Stockport.*

Lawrence Wong, aged 14

47 Reflections

If I could have my life again,
   what should I choose
   to lose
   of all its pain?

If I could live my life again,
   how should I plan
   the span
   of loss and gain?

If I could write once more my years,
   how would it seem –
   my scheme
   of hopes and fears?

If I could have my time again,
   I'd hope, dear God, to take
   whatever You might give,
   and leave
   my life for You to make
   in sun and rain.

Revd Peter Stokes, *of Newton Abbot, Devon*

48 Back to those old streets

Lord, I have today been back to those old streets
of childhood where nothing then, it seemed, had
space to breathe or time to spare; where growing
up was eager and the ways of age too far to fear;
where hope lay in departure and the leaving had
no saddened cry. And this day, Lord, I have been grateful
for my understanding of beginning, that in those
grey streets I began and learned Your blessing of the world You gave
and found for me the time to share.

Brian Parvin, *of Shrewsbury, Shropshire.*

49 On being given Buckfast Abbey fudge

This happy prayer was spontaneously offered from the back of a car as the author was being taken home following a day out.

The monks made this? Holy fudge.
Thank You, God, for this lovely fudge
And thank You, God, for making the monks who
Made this fudge. Amen.

Phoebe Argyle, *aged 6, of Auckland, New Zealand.*

Katherine Polland, aged 15

50 A way to know You?

Dear God (Higher Power, Source of Love, Spirit of the Universe),

Please help me to find a way to know You. A way that is comfortable. A way in which there is no fear of You.

Show me how to communicate with You in my spirit, in my conscience, in my heart. I am still confused and blind. I need to know You are there. Please make Yourself real and help me to understand Your mysterious ways.

I need Your help to get through this day. Help me to face everyone and everything that comes along with kindness, courage and wisdom and, if possible, a little serenity, please.

I pray for the things I want (but only if these are Your will for me) and I also pray for the ability to accept what You give me, because only You know what I need. Amen.

Sylvan Mason, *of south-west London.*

51

Lord, You know all my thoughts and my inmost feelings.
You know how much I love – yet I feel so helpless,
There seems to be a wall, I cannot break it down,
What must I do?
I so want to help carry this burden
But try as I might, I cannot succeed.
Is it perhaps
I want to control that which is not in my power?
Am I too impatient, wanting it my way, only my way?
Or is it
That You are telling me to put it into Your hands,
Trusting that You will show the way? Amen.

Vera Nicholson, *of Holbeach, South Lincolnshire.*

52 Lent prayer

Why do you wait for me to welcome you?
No worth of mine can recompense this trust.
How may I offer all that is your due,
Dust that I am? I shall return to dust.

My heart is narrow; – shall it find a place
For you to live in; honour such a guest?
Only if you would grant my prayer for grace
Could I afford a room where you might rest.

I slept too long; I have not watched an hour.
I did not hear you call me in the garden.
Yet I believe your mercy gives me power
To ask your blessing and receive your pardon.

Anne Rigg, *of Ealing.*

53 A prayer for commitment

Courage, please Lord, for overcoming fears,
Obedience to Thy will, in spite of tears.
Mastery of self in face of strong temptation,
Mercy and love in place of condemnation.
Integrity throughout the common day,
Truth, although it may be hard to say.
Ministry to follow up Thy teaching,
Example in the practice of the preaching.
Now, Lord, my life I give and pledge to Thee,
Thank You for all You give and promise me.

Daphne Paul, *of Kidlington, Oxford.*

54 Extempore prayer

Lord – just between you and me, I'm not very good at prayer
meetings and things. It's extempore prayer – you know, this off-
the-cuff stuff.

I'd rather write a proper prayer at home beforehand – one I'd
thought about carefully and had time to read through. One I'd be
proud to share.

But this is extempore stuff, Lord, so I suppose it wouldn't be fair.

Yes, Lord, I do know you prompt me with ideas and a desire to
speak out loud, but I feel silly and am afraid of making an
exhibition of myself.

Afraid someone else will start off at exactly the same time as me
and I'll be embarrassed. So, if it's all the same to you, I'll stick to
praying about the weather. They know it's my topic. No one else
ever prays about the weather at the prayer meetings. They
wouldn't want to tread on my feelings so I can feel confident I
won't tread on anyone else's toes.

I'll pray about the other things at home, I promise. Amen.

Janis Priestley, *of Lichfield, Staffordshire.*

55 Redeemed

I'm alone and deserted, lost and afraid, angry and fearful,
  I am searching for something, yet trusting in nothing.
    I laugh without humour and live without sharing.
        In a cynical world, what is left?
        Hope remains the key to life.
          God's love is on offer.
            What shall I say?
              I answer Yes,
                My Father
                God.

Zoë Crutchley and Veronica Parnell, *of Wolston, Warwickshire.*

56 Prayer for help

*Written on a pub counter in 1973 when the world seemed to have ended
and there was no one to talk to. Fortunately the author is still here to
tell the tale.*

I am lost, Father
and
in all the millions
who need You
and call to You,
I ask humbly,
Seek me
And find me
And end this anguish.

In this pain
That tears and disintegrates me,
Bring me peace,
And in my isolation,
My loneliness,
Send me
Tenderness, warmth and love.

In my despair
Send me hope
And promise for the future
And give direction,
Fulfilment,
To my life.

In my abject weakness
And my self-loathing,
Give me the strength,
The courage,
To do
What I have to do.
Make my life purposeful
And give meaning to my existence.

I am lost, Father.
Seek me
And find me
And end this anguish.

Reg Mares, *retired, of Marylebone, west London.*

57 My Father

Written while the author was still in the services.

My Father, let me bend my knee
In prayer and praise for love of Thee.
Let Thy helping hand be near
And take from me all thoughts of fear,
Granting courage, strength and love,
Through Thy Son, in Heaven above.
In Thy mercy, grant my prayer,
Which in my heart is always there,
That soon I shall be on my way
To my home and no more to stray.
To Thy servants Thou art Supreme
And speak to some, as in a dream,
But we who know Thee, live apart,
For Thou dwellest in each heart.
It is Thy work which covers all,
Hear, O God, then this my call.
Grant this prayer, in our Lord's Name,
To Him who died to save our shame,
Send me home to spend my life
Beside Thy servant I call, My Wife.

Mr Bert Herring, *of Bridgwater, Somerset.*

58

Dear God,
Thank You for the new day,
The first rays of sunshine
Stealing into my bedroom,
Illuminating my spirit
Left over from recent dreams
With love and joy – to be alive.
Thank You for another day.

Leslie B. Harmer, *of Bermuda.*

Oscar Viney, aged 15

59 Be with me

Dear Lord,
Please be with me.
I'm finding it hard to cope at the moment. I'm feeling alone and
    weary, and I need Your support to carry on.
Help me to sleep tonight, wrap me in that warm, soft blanket I call
    Your love and let me rest. Then, tomorrow, let me put my hand
    in Yours, and lead me through the turmoil of the next few days.
Thank You for being here with me, I know I do not deserve such
    unerring and unconditional love.
Thank You with all my heart.

Elizabeth Williams, *of Forest Gate, east London.*

60 I am full, Lord

This poem was written some years ago after the author was informed he had Parkinson's disease.

I am full, Lord,
Full of the raincloud
That has passed my way.
So much to do, so
Much love to share.
And there is a rainstorm,
Turning my work to clay.
As You can see, Lord,
I am full.

I am full, Lord,
Full of the uncertainty
That has passed my way.
So much to do, so
Much love to share.
And now my work seems ended,
Filling my heart with sadness.
As You can see, Lord,
I am full.

I am full, Lord,
Full of Your spirit
That gently washes my soul.
So much to do, so
Much love to share.
And there is that raincloud,
With sunbeams shining through.
As You can see, Lord,
I am full.

I am full, Lord,
full of the hope
That has come my way.
So much to do, so
Much love to share.
And now my work seems endless,
Filling my heart with gladness.
As You can see, Lord,
I am full.

Revd Peter Coppen, *of Greatworth, Oxfordshire.*

61 A preacher's prayer

O holy Spirit of God, come upon me now,
First for truth of doctrine,
Then for clarity of expression,
Then for warmth of communication
Then for power of persuasion,
And finally for the will to action,
That we may be doers of the Word.

Simon Baynes, *of Winkfield, Berkshire.*

62 Silence and peace

The sign on the door said 'Absolute Silence'
No welcome there, I thought.
So I opened the door with my preconceived ideas and my
judgement ready to judge.

I walked into 'Absolute Silence' and
Tiptoed to a pew.
I sat down and bowed my head and felt Your presence.

I bowed my head and I knelt down and I asked You to speak to me.
I heard nothing but the 'Absolute Silence'
But what I experienced was Your peace.

I looked up at the windows. The blue was the colour of a summer sky,
The gold of the icons glistened,
The flames of the candles flickered,
In the 'Absolute Silence' You listened.

How we love to enjoy our services,
How we love to chat and sing.
How much time do we find to talk to You in
'Absolute Silence'?

We try to fit You in, Lord, into our busy lives.
Sundays are convenient and perhaps one other night.
But when we need You, Lord, are we quite so understanding?
We expect You to be there when we call.
We expect our answers straight away,
We don't expect 'Absolute Silence'.

Eva Wherlock, *of Bedminster Down, Bristol.*

63 A prayer for kites

When flying a kite means fishing the sky
breath hangs bated for luck to nibble.
An act of faith takes shape in flight
and tugs at fibres in the brain to uproot
blossoming spires. It's a tool in service
of insight, a shield against invisible
pressures, a device of hectic tensions
tackling staves of unplayable music.
To keep hope afloat is a knack; it can't
be taught. You need a hilltop in the mind
and a hot line to dream dimensions;
enough slack between wish and will to lift
the buckling spirit, then you're on your own.
A mock visor can battle on behalf
of anyone, upholding bravado,
quickening pulses with racy stuff
that reaches everywhere like veins on a leaf.
It battles the swift. Let it dance itself
to tatters of heraldic frenzy, snapping
at clouds, bluffing a swoop on its shadow:
yet it seems purposeful, as if entreating
an end to suffering. May whatever kites
beseech be granted, since all of us pluck
out of the air more than was sent up.

Bill Turner, *of Lincoln.*

64

Good Lord, please help my unbelief.
You really do exist? Good Lord!

Charles Brien, *retired civil servant, of Poynton, Cheshire.*

65

Almighty, Absolute God,
How easy I find it to be convinced of Your presence. Daily, I am
aware of Your influence upon my psyche. Nightly, my body
sleeps, yet still my soul continues to dwell in the light of richly
symbolic worlds.

In contrast, there are those who seek You through the faculty of
intellect alone and thus remain confined to a gaze that does not
extend beyond the physical.

Therefore, I pray, O God, if You will grant me just one thing, then let that be wisdom, for it is in wisdom that I can share in Your vision of the universe, seeing it as it truly must be, interconnected and infinite.

Only through wisdom can I hope to attain a totality of mind and a soundness of judgement that transcends mere cleverness. And only from Your well can the waters of wisdom be drawn.

Leon Bambury, *of Mapperley, Nottingham.*

66 The blacksmith's prayer

Written with a blacksmith's son in mind who now, incidentally, is a church bell-ringer.

Fan, O Lord, the still small
   Flame In the hearts of Thy servants; that our
      Fire may consume the darkness, and
         Forge a new sword in your hand. Amen.

Andrew Sewell, *of Aldbourne.*

67 A prayer from God

You know, you are more precious than gold, than fine gold.
You know, you are surrounded by loved ones, family and friends.
You know, you are in my keeping, day and night, loved and cared
   for, always.
Draw on this wealth, and remember.

Myra Schofield, *of Berry Brow, Huddersfield.*

68

I'm sorry, God, but I've done it again. Two days gone by and I haven't spoken to You; or given You a chance to speak to me. I'm sorry. I really am sorry, and I'll try to do better.

There was that silly film on TV last night. Why did I watch it? I knew it was rubbish. And not even clean rubbish. So I went to bed tired without so much as a thank You, God, for another day.

But now I am saying sorry, and thank You. Thank You that You always give us another chance, and whenever we want to talk to You, there You are ready to listen; eager to listen. For You love Your foolish wandering children.

In the name of Jesus, I pray. Amen.

Eric Leat, *of Bookham, Surrey.*

69 Prayer for a loving heart

O Lord, give me a heart of compassion,
To put others' needs before my own.
Grant me the gift of humility, I pray,
That Your grace may be sufficient for me.

For in my weakness, Your strength is made perfect,
In my dependence, Your glory is displayed.
May I receive Your strength and wisdom,
Through Your Spirit who dwells in me.

O Lord, I pray for love and understanding
For the suffering and hurt souls of this world,
That I may be Your instrument of healing,
Your hands and feet and heart to serve.

May I bring lost souls to know You,
That they may feel Your tender loving care,
As in Your arms You enfold them,
Until in heaven Your peace we share.

Sylvia Williams, *retired teacher, of Boughrood, Brecon, Powys.*

70

Teach us, Lord,
How to love You.
All our lives
Never to leave You. Help us
Know that

Your way should be
Our way
Until the end of time.

Frank Keetley, *retired teacher, of Maltby, Rotherham.*

71

*A grace composed in the 1960s to replace the normal 'Benedictus',
creating a small consternation at the school in which it was introduced!*

May the death of the things we eat be justified by the life we live.

Revd Eric Ackroyd, *retired university lecturer, of Northampton.*

72

Lord, grant me grace,
To accept Your embrace.

Revd David Abel, *property developer, of Balcombe, West Sussex.*

73

Open my eyes and my mind and put a guard on my tongue.
Don't let me waste my thoughts, but put a song in my heart.
Thank You for Your blessings.

Angela Grant, *of Cucklington, Somerset.*

74

A hopeful prayer, and one which anticipates a 'Heavenly
   Banquet'.
Thank You God for chocolate cake.

Samantha Schad, *student, of South Croydon.*

75 Let me be like a mountain

Inspired from the heart by the mountains in Switzerland.

Let me be like a mountain,
Patient and strong,
And let my thoughts be like trees,
Growing upright on the steepest slopes.

Let my deeds be like fruits,
Dropping from those upright trees
Into the hands
In need of them.

Let my life flow
Like water from ice-clad rocks,
Like a brook through a stony gorge,
Like a river through a blooming valley,
Like a stream –
Slowly and safely carrying
Hours of pleasure
And hours of grief
To the ocean of eternity.
Amen.

Roland Mueller, *computer specialist, of Schoenaich, Germany.*

Hidetoshi Tomikami, aged 15

76

Lord, please help me to avoid degenerating into an avaricious money-accumulating machine, amassing as much as possible from each patient; especially from those that are 'easy-meat'.

You are in charge here.
Thank You, Father.

Alan Brooke, *retired dentist, of Oswestry, Shropshire.*

77 Working through disappointments

Lord God, you know they seemed so great –
   those many disappointments and frustrations
     which I met when hopes were high
      but now I see them as just part
   of a detailed plan for me.
I cannot tell what tomorrow holds
   of joy and laughter, pain and tears
     but offer thanks for what is past
     and when some things come back to haunt
   I clasp the hand of one who knows the way.

Randle Manwaring, *of Newick, East Sussex.*

78

Loving Father,
I am nothing other than that which
Thou art making me.

I have no powers other than those
which Thou hast given me.

Help me to use them according to Thy
will, that I may become exactly what
Thou desirest me to be: so that,
both here and hereafter, I may
perfectly fulfil the purpose for
which Thou art making me. Amen.

Revd Leo Straub, *of Tuckton, Bournemouth.*

79

Please God, let those that need me always be able to recognise me
and reach me, no matter how good or bad I feel inside.

Pat Caplin, *of Colchester.*

80 A new mother's prayer

Here is my new baby, Lord.
Fresh to life,
Fresh to me,
Fresh to my husband,
Fresh to the family.
Bless this new life
With health and strength,
To grow in Your love and wisdom.
Through our Lord Jesus Christ. Amen.

Margaret Loughran, *retired health visitor,*
of Headington, Oxford.

Derek Wing Hang Ho, aged 15

81 A short rhyme about Guildford Cathedral

I'm only a small cat at Guildford Cathedral,
But I think you'll agree my appearance is regal
And I'm told by St Francis the Good God does smile,
When I walk, tail erect, down the long centre aisle.

I'm the custodian's cat and privileged to go
Where mere mortals cannot, thus I'd like you to know
That many a field-mouse who crept to the altar
I've pounced on and eaten, and then after the slaughter

I've cast my eyes up to the Heavenly Father.
He understands all, but my master would rather
I ate from a tin. What an insult to cattery.
I'm lord of the jungle, an enemy to rattery.

So ladies and gentlemen, when next you see me
Purring around gartered leg at the Deanery,
Forgive all my misdeeds and realise that
I'm an acknowledged ecclesiastical cat.

Doreen Bufton, *of Norfolk.*

Ellie Pang, aged 14

82

Lord, I asked You for a fragrant flower
      And You gave me a shrivelled bulb.
I asked You for a harvest to reap,
      You put my hand to the plough.
I asked that I might bear fruit,
      And You gave me a handful of seed.
I asked You to build me a fire,
      And You handed me sticks and a flint.
I asked You to give me light
      And You gave me oil for my lamp.
I asked for a garland of joy
      And You wove me a crown of thorns...

Hazel Macfarlane-Grieve, *nurse, of Troon, Ayrshire.*

83 Mercy

Become the merciful drop of rain
    The angel of stone with her hands cupped high
    Her face is washed and worn away
Be a sign of life in a world of death
    That my flesh may be warm
    That I may learn to love and caress
Become compassion in the cooling shadow
    This window on the morning of my sorrow
    That I may break in the arms of another
Bring me back to the home you prepared long ago
Become a testament of truth
Lift words from a page and make them wise
Teach us to become one with each other
Before this day is over
Bring Your blessing to all the lost
But first bring it to me.

Paul Jones, *of Paignton, Devon.*

84 On retreat

This prayer was written at the Carmelite Priory, Boar's Hill,
near Oxford, a few months before the author's death on
St Cecilia's Day, 1996.

Why retreat, withdraw, draw back?
An entering into reality,
The reality of God's presence.
Stillness, can I cope?
Solitariness, still less –
Yet, enabled to let go,
His Presence is here,
Holding, carrying, enfolding
Within His everlasting arms.
Relax, let go –
With thanksgiving and serenity
Retreat into His love.

Margaret Bryden, *a professional cellist, of Torquay, Devon.*

85 Living water

Lead us, Lord God, from the stagnant
Pool of sin to streams of living water:
To draw from the well of life, to drink
From the cup of salvation, to taste
From the river of repentance, and to
Bathe by the lakeside of love; that,
Having thirsted after righteousness
on earth, we may find our spirits filled
From that fountain of forgiveness in
Heaven; through the grace of Jesus
Christ our Lord.

Revd W. Gerald Jones, *Church of Scotland minister, of Maybole, Ayrshire.*

86 The waves

Written after the death of a loved one.

O, my God,
I am floundering!
All my supports have been swept away
And I am drowning in the depths of the sea.
O, let me walk upon the water
As Jesus did.
Amen.

Jennifer Hannigan, *of Selly Oak, Birmingham.*

Lawrence Wong, aged 14

87 Bats in the roof

I have bats in my roof. At first I was not pleased,
but they are a protected species. So I had to preserve them.
Then I started reading about them, and I rather got to like
the fascinating creatures. Now I am happy, even
proud, to have them in my roof. But I would not want them
in my living room. They are alright as long as they stay
in their place.

Then I realised – That's how I treat You, Lord.
I may know all about You, but do I really know You?
I may be happy, even proud, to be associated with You.
But I want to keep You in Your place – where You cannot
invade my comfort, where You cannot change my life.

The bats are happy with my roof space. It meets their needs.
But will You be happy until You come into every room?
I think I know the answer, Lord.

John Whiteley, *accountant, of Kilmington, Devon.*

Oscar Viney, aged 15

88 In memory of a dear mother

Dearest Lord,
Who instructed me to love my neighbour as myself,
Teach me to love myself –
A love not born of vanity or self-esteem
But springing solely from the knowledge that I'm your creation.
Help me always to do my best in all things –
And, that done, grant me the peace of mind which is my due.
There will be days I feel I could have done better
And there will be better days when I do just that.
But when I've done my best – and I'm only human –
Then let me sleep peacefully at night.
And if I stray and offend you
Be assured of my love for you – even at the instant of my weakness.
Let me also be constantly aware of your infinite forgiveness
That I might never suffer the agonies of total despair.
Help me to foster a 'best friend' relationship with you,
Recognising that sometimes even best friends have their differences.
And when I've grown to accept my shortcomings
And realise what a truly powerful thing it is to be plain average –
Then will I be able to love my neighbour as myself
In a manner my neighbour might appreciate.
Amen.

Francis Norton, *quantity surveyor, of West Derby, Liverpool.*

89 For a safe journey

*This prayer was composed for use when on a car journey. The author
and his family use the first five lines whenever they travel.*

With angels and archangels
And with all the company of heaven,
Keep us safe on this journey.
Make us mindful of the needs of others
And them of us.
Help us to e thankful for our car
And all the care that has gone
Into making it roadworthy.
Enable us to spot if it is not so
For the safety of everyone.
While concentrating on the road and the traffic,
Give us the gift of being aware
Of our beautiful world
And of being thankful.

When the environment is not beautiful,
Enable us to pray for what we notice
And to work to make things better.
As we arrive at our destination,
Give us time to relax and enjoy where we are.
May we cherish the place and appreciate
That we are all on a journey
And that everything is lent to us.
We acknowledge that while we may feel
That we own things,
In fact it is all lent to us
For the benefit of all, to Your glory.
Indeed Lord, may we read the map of life
Accurately, with Your love and presence. Amen.

Revd Peter Thomas, *of Bromley, Kent.*

90 Thoughts of a new grandad

Welcome, newborn grandchild,
To a world of wondrous options
Which none the less has lost its way
At times it seems.
It can be a difficult place these days.
Perhaps it always was, is, and will be;
Each time to be born unique,
Each circumstance unrepeatable.

My prayer for you is this:
That you throughout your days may have a God
(I sometimes fear not everybody has)
Not just any old god; your very own
To guide you through your days
To help you with your choices
To calm you when fears of the unaccustomed assail you
To raise doubts, doubtless,
But to help you plot a correct course
With certainty.
Think hard, choose wisely,
Seek beauty, find the best,
Be happy and enjoy.

Beware a wicked world: yet there is love –
May you be fortunate to find it
And may your God
Your very own God
Grant you peace.

Colin Russell, *retired insurance broker, of Colton, Leeds.*

91 The squashed grape

You trod on me, God.
I know You didn't mean to,
I got in the way –
Just the other day –
You trod on me, God.

It wasn't your fault
(or mine for that matter)
what a splatter
squash – flat.
You trod on me, God,
and that's that.

But how now?
I know you care, aware,
and I need to get up.
It's no fun being flat,
and I am right down,
squashed flat.
A lot of people are
treading on me now
so how about that?

Listen to me, get it right.
Who do you think you are? God said.
Listen, I need you as wine
You were a grape off my vine,
I pressed you flat in my vat.

Oh that's fine, I said,
that's fine.
And God said: *You can forget the pain*
and be champagne.
Champagne? I said to God
Am I that good?
Yes, said God, *That's understood,*
You're the best wine
When you are mine.

Anne Shells, *retired, of Glastonbury,*
Somerset.

Katherine Polland, aged 15

92 Imago Dei (Image of God)

To be said slowly, pausing after each section, and repeated several times.

Lord God, who made me in your image,
give me wisdom;

Lift up my thoughts
and carry them ahead of me;

Gather and straighten my emotions
and direct them towards you;

Raise my being
ever nearer to your own;

Lord God, help me to become
a clearer image of you.

Amen.

John Haldane, *a professor of philosophy, at the University of St Andrews, Fife.*

93 A traveller's prayer

The author composed this prayer in 1953 and thereafter used it every year for over 30 years while travelling with parties of boys to Switzerland. It was used for evening prayer, held in the biggest of the hotel's bedrooms, each night.

O God, the Father of all men, who watchest over all creatures that move upon the face of the earth, grant that we who now travel together may be always in Thy safe keeping; that our ways be Thy ways; and that at the end of life's journey we may find a safe home in the love of Thy Son, our Saviour, Jesus Christ our Lord. Amen.

Barry W. Johnson, *a retired schoolmaster, of Hurstpierpoint, West Sussex.*

94 The child

A child.
The light of hope shining bright in her young eyes;
Hope for the future.
Hope and love.
Trust for parent and friend,
Even for stranger.

But look what we have done.
We have extinguished that flame of hope,
Perverted the trust and love.

No longer can the child play,
Happy and carefree.
She knows hurt and pain,
Rejection.

They have been robbed of their youth.
Their innocence.
They are told that they are worthless.
Treated as garbage.
They are abused –
Mentally, physically.

Why do we do this?
Why? Oh why?

A child.
Just another symptom of a fallen world?
A child.
Loved by God.
By God who commanded us
'Come as little children.'
By God who calls us his children.

God –
Father –
Forgive us –
For every young life
Battered and bruised.
Father, forgive us.
Forgive us.

Alan Darlington, *of Barton-on-Humber, North Lincolnshire.*

95 In memory of a father

This prayer was composed after the death of the author's father, Cyril.

G is for the guidance you showed us every day
R is for reassurance you gave along the way
E is for for encouragement in the things we would do
A is for for avice, we would always come to you!
T is for the tenderness whenever we did cry.
Now it's time to leave us, it's hard to say "Goodbye"
Your life with us is over, it's time for you to rest
We just want you to know Dad, you really were the best
Yes, you were a GREAT Dad, we're proud of you,
you see
Your strength is all around us,
It's called "Our Family".

Julie Gunther, *of Bromley, Kent.*

96 Prayers for the one at home

Lord, here I stand swirling the soapsuds,
Watching the dirt disappear,
Seeing the sunlight held in the bubbles.
I reflect, Lord, that this is how you deal with me,
Pouring your love into my life,
Living water, washing away the dirt, the sin.
Filling me with the radiance of light.
Lord, keep me swirling.

I'm tired, Lord, tired of ironing,
I hate standing here smoothing creases from sheets and shirts,
Folding, pressing, airing.
I've lots of questions, 'Why me? Who cares?'
I don't want to press the point, Lord, but I'm fed up.
Now I've aired my views so take me now,
Help me fold my hands and listen, Lord,
Smooth my troubled heart. Amen.

Here I am again, Lord, washing the floor –
Dirty footprints, muddy paws, grubby marks.
What a mess other people make.
Here's an impression of mine with someone's overlapping;
So I think, Lord, how I cannot avoid
Other people stepping into my life,
And I into theirs.
Lord, help me to live so that the impressions I make
Will show only your love.

It's time for stove cleaning, Lord,
Here I am, dirty, dishevelled,
Asking myself, why don't I clean up more often?
Well, why don't I, Lord?
Why do I let my failures, my disappointments,
My grubby sins accumulate?
Why don't I let you clean me up more often?
Lord cleanse me now. Amen.

It's marmalade-making time, Lord,
The kitchen is full of steam and smells;
I mix things and smell oranges and sugar, and ponder.
How odd it is that it needs both bitter and sweet together
To make something good and wholesome.
Come into my life, Lord,
Take the bitter things
And use them in your plan for me,
To make something new, useful, sweet and wholesome. Amen.

Dorothy Jamal, *of Wells, Somerset.*

97 How strange

How strange it is
That life goes on
Year after year, after year.
How strange that luck
Can change for the best
When suddenly death draws near.
How strange to find faith
How strange to find hope
How strange to want to remain
When before you wanted to be gone.
Strange the world will always be,
The same year after year.
How strange it feels to find the will
To start fighting over again.

Sheila Wall, *of Leicester.*

98 Bread (for the day)

Matthew 6:9–13.

Lord,
forgive us
our daily bread.
Whether we have
thick, thin or
medium sliced,
while other men
would crave –
a crust.
Starving eyes
hunger for that
last stale slice;
their distant
pleadings heard
in our excesses.
Crumbs
from our tables
would satisfy
their needs.
Another sandwich,
piece of toast
or empty plate?

Multiple choices
greet me this morning –
Lord,
forgive me
my daily bread.

Sandra Woodman, *of Ardleigh, Colchester.*

99 For the times

For the times I walked in danger
And you gently led me through...
For the times you have protected me
And I never even knew...

For the times I faced decisions
And you showed me which way to go...
For the times when I was tempted
And you softly whispered 'No'.

How can I ever thank you
For your everlasting care?
I don't know I deserve it
But you're with me, always there.

Margaret Wright, *of Kingsley, Northampton.*

100 The death of a child

*The pain at the loss of one's child remains forever. A horrific event like
Dunblane restirs all that hurt and suffering. This prayer, written in
response to the author's personal tragedies in 1974 and 1975, has been
circulated to many other parents who have suffered similar losses since.*

As they approach the dread of night
Whose darkness is the horror of that day;
As they confront their failure to protect
Or even offer comfort in the dying;
As they cry 'There is no God –
Or if there is I hate him'

    O God, in your absence, walk with them.

As they cling to the umbilical cord
Severed once yet still attached;
As they grieve, not for themselves,
But for their child's loss;
As they cry 'There is no Heaven –
Or if there is why am I not there too?'

    O God, in their suffering, let their love be at peace.

As they waken in the morning
And in those brief Spring moments
Forget;
As truth forces its way into their minds
But their hearts refuse to believe;
As reality cruelly dawns and there is no escaping

O God, in their weeping, share their pain.

As they move through that dark tunnel which is the future
In fear that each step will take them further from their love;
As they walk blindly forward,
Heavy footed, blinkered, no questions left to ask;
As they sing no songs and laugh no laughter –
Or if they do, despise themselves for it

O God, in their despair, bring hope.

Elizabeth Miles Chester, *company director, of Kingsdown, Bristol.*

101 A churchwarden's prayer

This prayer was triggered by the comment 'Awesome' by an American visitor to the Church of St James the Greater in Stanford Bishop, Herefordshire.

LORD, we've been landed with an ancient Church set amidst fields rather than houses. The worshippers are few, the repairs are many, the money is tight.
Then, one hot summer's evening, we await the visiting priest and glance over the visitors' book...

'Lovingly cared for'

'An oasis of peace and heaven on earth'

'A joy to visit'

'Awesome'

Humbled, we put aside our material worries and vow anew to keep our Church open and unlocked.

Lord, may we never again think of closing the door. Give us always the strength and the means to keep open this house of prayer. Amen.

Frank E. Hulme, *farmer and churchwarden, of Herefordshire.*

102 Let me be devout

Let me be devout but not pious,
questioning but not cynical;

Let me be merry but not unseemly,
proper but not prim;

Let me be innocent but not ingenuous,
wise but not clever;

Let me be single-minded but not narrow,
amenable but not pliant;

Let me be precise but not petty,
unworldly but not unthinking;

Let me be detached but not aloof,
compassionate but not sentimental;

Let me be quick but not hurried,
patient but not apathetic;

Let me be generous but not indulgent,
tolerant but not permissive;

Let me be relaxed but not slothful,
diligent but never too busy.

Fill me with joy but not frivolity;

Teach me trust but not credulity;

Show me grief but not self-pity;

Give me peace but never ease.

Oliver J. A. Leech, *teacher, of Newcastle under Lyme, Staffordshire.*

103 My heart is hot within me

The following was previously published in The Bell, *a free town magazine, in the Arundel area.*

I am angry, Lord,
Hot is my heart against them,
The scoffers, the destroyers and molesters.
They hurt the aged and the young.
I hate the deeds, the words and lack of words,
Refusal to love, to look at You.
My heart is hot against the ones who use Your name
    and yet deny You.

They say, 'It was all so long ago and what is the Truth?'
Some say You are dead, or never lived and never healed, and will
    not now.
My heart is hot against them.
I am not another Elijah.
Help me to forgive.
I too have sinned against You.
I too have not believed.
Forgive me, O my Lord!
Help me never to give up.
Help me to love with Your love. Amen.

Emilie Bruell, *of Arundel, West Sussex.*

104 Prayer for everyone

Help us, Lord, to pray in gentle tones
As soft as snowflakes falling on the ground.
Our words will light upon the air
And rise to Thee in form of prayer.
Console us with your loving ways,
Fill our heads with Kindly joy.
When our bodies' work is done
And we lie beneath the earth,
Lift us from this world of care
Give us grace to be with Thee
In heaven above, eternally. Amen.

Francis B. Rylance, *a retired schoolmaster, of Wigan, Lancashire.*

105 Don't listen to me, Lord

The author was inspired to write this prayer by an illness which had prevented her from working for six years.

Don't listen to me, Lord
    when my prayer is full of self-pity.
When I approach You in arrogance
    take no heed of me, Lord.

When my heart is stained with selfishness
    as I forget to count my blessings,
When my own needs take precedence,
    suffer me not, Lord.

When my tears fall in anger
   and not heartfelt repentance,
When I voice my indignation
   in Your mercy, hear it not.

When I ask 'Why, oh why?'
   and struggle to understand
When I fail to trust and follow
   take no notice of me, Lord.

Lest I should lose Your precious love
   when I reject my Cross
   complaining, 'it's too heavy'
   don't listen to me, Lord.

Efrosyni Hobbs, *of Plumstead, London.*

106 In times of stress

In times of stress, dear God, we turn to you
To find some comfort, seems the only way,
Our selfish plea that troubles may come right
Is our sole thought as we kneel down to pray.

We take for granted all the lovely things
Which you have given, that we may enjoy,
The pretty flowers and majestic trees
That dot the countryside beneath the sky.

The animals, the birds that sing on high –
The landscape is a carpet hued in green –
The mountainsides that sweep down to the sea
Add further to this panoramic scene.

To give our thanks for all these wondrous gifts –
Amidst our daily chores we may forget –
Dear Lord, we ask, forgive our selfishness,
Make us appreciate our massive debt.

Instead of thinking only of ourselves,
Encourage us to give our thanks to you.
We have not yet your pure and selfless mind,
Forgive us Lord, we know not what we do.

Wally Olney, *of Enfield, London.*

107 Blessing

May the Love of God enfold you,
    the Strength of God uphold you,
    and the Peace of God be in your heart.

May the Angels of God guard you,
    the Saints of God pray for you,
    and the Blessing of God,
    Father, Son and Holy Spirit
    be with you now and always. Amen.

Revd Michael Payne, *of Happisburgh, Norwich.*

108

Remind me that I am not turning my anger at others in onto myself
But rather the reverse, as I turn my self-hate out onto others.
Forgive me my conceit when I say I was created in your image
And again when I recreate you in mine.
It is all part of my desperate need to know that you hear me,
For who else will listen to me more willingly than I do myself?
As much as I believe in myself, I doubt also
And so when I believe in you, I doubt.

Give me the strength and reconfirm my belief that I am
communicating with you and not talking to myself.

When I go to war against others rather than face the battles inside me
Give me the resolution, the will, the strength to fight and win
    my inner war,
That I may love and be at peace with my fellows.

Peter Hall, *of Bovey Tracey, Devon.*

109 Hands

Hands touching in prayer
Pointing upwards to the sky,
Taut, tapering, beautiful fingers
Beseeching God the most high

To grant us his wisdom
To fill out our knowledge of science
Of the evolution of our being
With spirituality and prescience.
Of things unknown, beyond reason,
The presence of God's stillness,
Grant us imagination and the power,
God, to heal man's illness.

Dorothy Engels, *of Harrogate, North Yorkshire.*

110 Tapestry

Dear Lord, I praise and thank you
    for the life you've given me,
For my home and work and leisure,
    for my friends and family.
I thank you for the gifts
    that you have given me to share,
I praise you for the beauty
    that surrounds me everywhere.

And, though I never find this
    such an easy thing to do,
I praise you for the sad times
    and the difficulties, too –
For even when things happen
    that I cannot understand,
I know the pattern of my life
    is woven by your hand.

So help me, loving Father,
    never, never to complain
If among the strands of colour
    there are darker shades of pain.
I only see a few loose threads;
    You see the whole design...
So I praise you and I thank you
    for the tapestry that's mine.

Barbara Cunliffe, *of Heckmondwike, West Yorkshire.*

111 Prayer for bereavement

The author wrote this prayer after her daughter's suicide.

Dearest Lord, thank You for each new day,
Thank You for the gift to pray,
You have helped me in my hour of need,
Your love has sown the inquietous seed.
As I explore your wondrous ways,
You have lifted me out of my grieving haze,
All the knowledge that You impart,
All the love that is in your heart,
For all your children's erring ways,
If only they knew how You would brighten their days.
If only they knew of the love that You bear,
As their load You want to share.
If they could open their hearts and let You reside,
Then through life, your love would them guide.
Dearest Lord, thank You for all the gifts you impart,
Thank You for entering my grieving heart.

Joan Needham, *of Seaford, East Sussex.*

112 Dear Father...

Father, I know I am not really supposed to say things like this but
I am scared of dying. When will it happen? Ten years? Twenty
years? Next week? If I die suddenly then I'll have no time to tidy
up my house, and what will people think about the mess? I feel
quite all right at the moment but what about the years to come?
What if I get knocked down?

Will I feel much pain? I don't really like injections and things...
where will I die, anyway – at home or in hospital or in the garden?

Then the world will carry on without me and I'll soon be
forgotten. Life has to go on, everyone says.

It all worries me. We all have to die sometime, I know. I believe
that when I die I'll be with you in heaven. I'm not scared about
that – because I love You. No, I'm not scared of death – it's the
dying that worries me!

Give me peace to calm the panic within me and help me relax.
Help me to walk with you day by day. Help me to trust you until
the end of life and beyond.

For Christ's sake. Amen.

Revd Barbara Huntley, *Baptist minister, of Chadwell Heath, Romford.*

113 The listening loving God

O Lord,
You have the world in Your hands but You let us talk to You at
any time. Thank You that You are never too busy to listen and that
You are always available.

You know what we are going to say before we say it but You allow
us freedom to choose our own words. Thank You for free choice.

You are all-powerful but You allow us to look after Your world.
Thank You for Your patience and long-suffering when we make
mistakes.

Lord, we are such a small part of Your universe but You have given
us such an important job here. We can never thank You enough for
all You have done and for all that You will do for us in the future.

You knew what it was like to suffer when Your son died on the
cross; You know what it is like to feel sad and angry.

Lord, we offer thanks for Your faithfulness and love. We pray for
forgiveness and for our mistakes. We are small beings in a large
world – thank You Lord for being with us at all times.

In Your name we pray,

Amen.

Miss Avril Mann, *of Chadwell Heath, Romford, Essex.*

114 Christos, Son of the Father

Thou, Christos
Son of the Father
Figure of His substance
Son of the Mother
Thee, I adore.
I, separate yet unseparate
Throwing bread on the waters
I, returning ever to Thee
Inseparable from Thee
Yet bound to flow out as I,
Darkened only through ignorance
Illumined only by Thee
Thee only do I adore
Logos, the Verb.
Thou I see in all men
I, as man, function only in Thee.

Alice Hoffmann de Visme, *retired teacher, of North London.*

115 Graces

Dear Father, forbid that our gratitude
Should become the merest platitude.
   We delight in the food
   And the company's good,
    So help us to fulfil every beatitude.

Revd Toddy Hoare, *of Thirsk, North Yorkshire.*

116 Panic in the face of change

God, my higher power, I feel incarcerated by fear and uncertainty.
I feel alone in the darkness.
But I have to hang on to the faith
   that You have the key to my freedom,
   that your presence can replace my fears and calm my
   apprehensions.
Experience whispers that I have to be patient,
   because of my recognition of your offered hand leading me to
   calm,
And my vision of the way ahead
   will need to be refocused, having been unfocused by this panic.
I await in all trustfulness your cleansing of my spiritual eyes,
   your restoring of my undermined strength.
Forgive my doubting of your love,
   my loss of confidence in your care. Amen.

Fr Adrian Walker, *of the Isle of Dogs, London.*

117 Mental illness

Heavenly Father,
We pray for your mercy and strength for all those who are struggling
with any form of mental illness – whether minor or severe.

We pray that your Holy Spirit will stand alongside all who know
the isolation of this suffering. Help them when they feel that no
one understands or they cannot explain their feelings to anyone.
Draw near when they cannot find anyone to listen or people seem
to imply that it is their own fault.

We pray for those whose grip on reality fluctuates; help them to
discern what is true and take away the disturbing thoughts that
come into their minds and make them fearful.

Please bring them into contact with those who can help them –
those practising medicine, counsellors, and clergy. Give their
helpers a real insight into their needs and guide them as to what
should be done for each person.

For Jesus' Sake. Amen.

Anne Metherell, *of Worthing, West Sussex.*

118 Rest peacefully

I hope you are resting peacefully
In the spot where I had you laid,
I only visited you once I know
But no more could I have gone.
Although you've gone, away from my side
I know you're not there alone,
Others too are laid all around you
So you needn't be so afraid.
While you are resting
You'll have no pain
I wouldn't waken you, to suffer again,
So rest peacefully my friend.

Sheila Wall, *of Leicestershire.*

119 Silent contemplation

*Written by an Anglican discovering peace and joy in silent
contemplation of a talk delivered by a Quaker.*

Lord, in the silence we are aware of your presence
Working in our hearts,
Telling us things we never have time to hear.
To be still and know that You are God.
Comforting, consoling, challenging,
Christ of the now.
Fill our hearts with your perfect love.
In silent humility we dwell in your glory,
Receive your blessing,
Rejoice in your love.
Refreshed, renewed, redeemed.

Mavis Laybourn, *of Heelands, Milton Keynes.*

120 Prayer poem

Lord God,
I tried to write a prayer
But what is there to say?
'Please keep me in Your care
For just another day'!

Why only me, O Lord
When all the world
Is so in need of You?
I know that You love everyone
So what should my prayer do?

I think I'll just say 'Thank You',
Thanks that I know You're there,
Know You're in my daily life,
Know You're everywhere.

So Thank You God, for being
Everywhere for everyone,
Please teach the whole wide world to love You
That Your will may be done.

Joyce Goldie, *of Truro, Cornwall.*

121 Prayer for panic attacks

Dear Father, wrap me safely in the cocoon of your love for the
next few minutes. Soothe my anxious spirit and stop me doing
anything foolish. Help me to emerge into the world again, calm
and unafraid, and make me remember that I am surrounded by
your love, minute by minute, today and for every day until the
ending of my life.

Jean McKenzie, *retired secretary and occasional writer, of Manchester.*

122 Thank you, dearest Father

Thank you, dearest Father, for my wife.
Her selfless and generous nature reflects the
Generosity of your life on earth. Her love and
Devotion are more than I deserve. Your love
for me is shown in her patience with all my faults
and failings. You have answered all my prayers
in my wife, beauty, humour, wisdom, strength and
courage – tenderness and warmth and passion too.

I take her too much for granted as I treat your
love for me, my dearest Father. Help me to show
her in the little ways how much I love her,
let me lose my self-interest for her sake. Make me
someone worthy of her and our children. Teach me
your way of selflessness and generosity to my
precious treasure, my wife, my family, and help me
to the end.

Lieutenant Colonel Denis O'Leary OBE, MC *(retired), of Ely, Cambridge.*

123 A prayer for special people

Whoever I am with,
Whatever I am doing,
Wherever I am,
Whenever...
    let me be valued
    let me be dignified
    let me be respected
  as a unique human being.

Flo Longhorn, *education consultant in special needs, of Ingeldorf,
Luxembourg.*

124 Variation on a theme: The Lord's Prayer

Father,
Heaven's Keeper,
Your Grace crushes.
Pitch your tent here.
Give light to our paths,
Let them mirror a holy Way.
Set bread to nourish, wine to quench.
Score out what has gone awry,
Likewise we for evildoers.
Keep us from temptation,
Unite sin's thongs.
Glory's Yours
Always.
Amen.

Derek H. Webster, *NSM priest, of St Peter's Church, Cleethorpes and
lecturer at the University of Hull.*

125

A prayer written amidst the ruins of a first marriage, at the point where a special lady entered into the author's life. She became his second wife.

Lord, be with us in the dark
And calm the terror lurking in our minds;
    And when we fail, remember
    That we love you.

Lord, be with us in the light
And touch with sight the lidded eye that seeks;
    And when we fail, remember
    That we love you.

Lord, be with us in our minds
And colour thought with colours you have made;
    And when we fail, remember
    That we love you.

Lord, be with us in our lives
And shape our days with your creating hands;
    And when we fail, remember
    That we love you. Amen.

Chris J. P. Smith, *English teacher and writer, of Redhill, Nottingham.*

126 Spirit of God at the time of Pentecost

Spirit of God, be gentle with me.
Spirit of God, you are Cloud, and Wind and Fire,
Spirit of God, be gentle with me.

Spirit of God, your Cloud dims the Light, and I am in the dark;
        your Wind blows icily, and my heart is chilled;
        your Fire burns, and I am reduced to ashes.

Spirit of God, come, come once more, but,
Spirit of God, be gentle with me.

Sprit of God, may your Cloud shield my eyes from glare;
        may your Wind refresh me;
        may your Fire glow within me.

Sprit of God, be gentle with me.

God of Abraham, Isaac, and Jacob, at the time of Pentecost you gave to their descendants the Law.

Lord of the Apostles, Peter, James, and John, at the time of Pentecost you sent to their brethren the Holy Spirit whose gifts are love, joy, and peace.

Father of all time, at this time of Pentecost, fill all mankind with your same Spirit, making us so love your Law, that we may know too your peace and joy.

Margaret Brodie, *of south-west London.*

127

O, God, help me understand
That I am wholly, always
In your hand,

When soft living hardens me
To the needs of others
Focus me.

O, Creator, help me taste
This earth's freshness without worry,
Without haste.

And as the welcome petals
Of dawn bring light, let me hear
How truth settles.

O, Almighty, in your palm
Hold me ever free from fear
And from harm:

When the night is dark and deep
Wrap Heaven around me
While I sleep.

In your fingers, Father, I place
My soul for the touch of grace.

Joan Board, *of Retford, Nottinghamshire.*

128 A thank-you prayer

Thank you for my Mum and Dad,
Thank you for my food.
Thank you for me,
    and my brother and sister.
Thank you for the sun and moon.
Thank you, Lord, for everything. Amen.

Chris Norman, *aged 10, of the Junior Boys' Brigade Company, Leicestershire.*

129 A prayer on hearing midnight strike

O Bless the day that's gone, dear God,
And that which is to be.
And bless the day,
Whene'er it dawn,
When my soul comes to Thee.
And turn not then,
Thy face from me,
A sinner tho' I am.
Because between my sins and Thee
There stands Thy Holy Lamb.
That Holy One who died for me,
Whose flesh was riv'n
Whose soul was torn in agony
That I may get to Heav'n.
To Heaven where that very Lamb
Is thron'd in glory high
And whose beloved countenance
I hope
To see the day I die.

Hilda Kimber, *member of the Anglican Catholic Church, of Whickham,
Newcastle upon Tyne.*

130 A gardener's prayer

Hard on my knees, O Lord, I pray
And give you thanks for each new day.
And when the labours are all done
I'll render them to thy dear Son.

Lord, grant that I may live to be
Steadfast and patient as a tree,
With roots held firm while branches bend
Whate'er the trials on me descend.

Prune out the weak and useless part
To leave a pure and constant heart.
Plant thou within me from above
A stronger faith, and hope and love.

David Gray, *self-employed gardener, of Lewes, East Sussex.*

Fenn Chapman, aged 15

131 A prayer during illness

Lord, I don't quite know how to put this,
    if I did, I wouldn't have the problem I've got.
You see, Lord, I'm having trouble praying,
    finding the right words I mean,
    making sense of how I feel
    so that you can do something about it.
You must have noticed, Lord;
You are all seeing, all knowing.

It's been creeping up on me for some time,
    as my illness has gone on.
I never used to have trouble praying;
    you remember?
You have answered so many of my prayers in the past,
    not always in the way that I expected them to be answered,
    but answered nevertheless.
I can't ever remember doubting that you would.
Anyway, it's there in black and white in the Bible,
    and I believe in the Bible.

But lately it's been difficult...
    hard to explain really.
You see, Lord, I've used up all the prayers
    I can think of
    and nothing seems to be happening.
It's gone on for a long time, Lord.

Don't get me wrong, I know you can heal me, Lord.
And if it is your will,
  you will do so.
  When the time is right.

No, the trouble is me, Lord.
I seem to have come up against something
  like 'writer's block',
  except that in this case
  it's more like a 'prayer's block',
  and it's starting to bother me
  almost as much as my illness.
I could cope pretty well with the hurting
  when it was easier to pray.
Does this happen when the pain gets really bad, Lord?

I used to live each day expecting the next one
  to bring some improvement,
  my strength gained through prayer. Not so now;
  my time of prayer has become like a vacuum.

Without that strengthening prayer, Lord, I've come
  to feel that I'm nothing more than a case file,
  put back in a cabinet and forgotten
  as soon as I walk out of the doctor's surgery.
I'm being unfair... but you get like that after a while,
  and cynicism blends easily with pain.

I suppose that what I am asking of you, Lord,
  is that you will help me get back to praying
  in the way that I used to be able to pray
  and that you will 'renew a steadfast spirit within me',
  as the psalmist put it.
I think I need a sort of refresher course in praying.
You know what I mean, Lord,
Who could possibly know better what I mean?

Derek Robinson, *of Stratton, Dorchester, Dorset.*

132 Morning prayer

This prayer grew out of the author's faltering attempts to bring some structure to an otherwise shambolic period of prayer and reflection in early morning.

Holy God,
help me to experience your presence today
as creator, mother, father;
lover of all things and of all people.

Fire me with your spirit of truth and justice so that I may act with integrity, courage and openness

Inspire me with your spirit of wisdom and discernment so that I may know and hold fast to things of lasting value.

Excite me with your spirit of generosity and encouragement so that I may seek and foster the best in and for those I meet.

Fill me with your spirit of compassion and forgiveness so that I may grow in kindness, understanding, patience and self-control

I ask for your blessing on the people and
situations I will encounter in the course of
today: [*names*]

In the name of Jesus, may your loving,
creative spirit uphold us all
and strengthen us
to live and work for you.
Amen.

Nigel Walsh, *hospital planning director*, *of Ide, Exeter, Devon.*

133 In search of God

O God, why is it that I can't find You in the places that 'they'
say I should...
in cold church pews
in candles and stained glass?

There is no peace or challenge for me in liturgy and dogma.
The language of ages past leaves me standing, cold
and alone, as does the happy-clappy, 'Let's praise
the Lord' brigade.

I want to feel You, O God, deep within my spirit, within my soul.
I want to feel you
as a pulse that tingles
as a soothing balm that strokes and heals
as a prick to my conscience
as a sigh of contentment.

Help me not to feel guilty at leaving venerated objects and ancient words behind. Help me in my struggle to move on and explore, to be still, and silent... so silent that I could hear a white mist move in the early morning air.

Slow me down, help me to let go... and stop. So that I may hear and feel You in unexplainable ways.

Janet Brinsmead, *housewife, of Neath Hill, Milton Keynes, Buckinghamshire.*

134 Prayer for health

This prayer was compiled by a rabbi while serving in South Africa, and sent to members and friends who were very ill. The last three lines are derived from Psalm 31, and the first three from the Book of Common Prayer.

Heal us, O Lord, and we shall be healed; save us and we shall be saved; grant us a perfect healing from all our wounds. Blessed is the Lord, Healer of the sick.

Our God and God of our Fathers:

In my great need I pour out my heart to You:

The days and weeks of suffering are hard to endure, and I reach out for the help that only You can give.

May sickness and strain not weaken my faith, nor lessen my love, and from these trials that test me, may I gain a better appreciation of life's gifts, a deeper awareness of my blessings and a more sensitive sympathy and understanding for all in pain.

Into his hands I entrust my spirit, when I sleep and when I wake; and with my spirit, and my body also; the Lord is with me, I will not fear.

Rabbi Herbert Richer, *now retired, of The Gardens, St Julians, Malta and formerly of Temple Israel, Johannesburg.*

135 I sing alone softly

This was recently read aloud at Chichester Cathedral by a friend of the author.

Thou, Lord of marvel and mystery
And if all that hides itself from me,
Then so art thou Lord of the hiding,
The eyes that cannot lift to the horizon
Thou, Lord of their crying.

Then take what is yours,
The grief of the tears, the lameness of body,
The hundred bereavements, and all loss.
The house empty,
And what emptiness is.

I sing alone softly, and rock like a baby,
Thou art the alone, the grey day,
The silence in my soul.
So I sing to myself, like a mother.
I know no other way to still my fear.

Thou, Lord of the stone at my feet,
Am I as that small mass?
What is it to you, that stone?
I sing my song to it, and alone,
Like thou, it answers in silence.

Yet still thou art Lord of the song I sing
To stop my heart breaking.

Lillian Trueman, *of Fishbourne, Isle of Wight. Before retirement, she had 'almost every job there is', from washing up to teaching social studies.*

136 The shadow of Your wings

Last night I rested in Your love.
Peace fell round my shoulders like
a cloak of feathers.
Today I strove to do great things
and only fell ashamed and
seemingly alone.
Why do I listen, Lord, then disobey?
Put self first, shutting out the still, small voice?
In my vanity and pride I have become
yet again, wounded world-weary.
Forgive my waywardness.
Bring me back home to You
where I belong.
And let me once more rejoice in
the shadow of Your wings.

Alison Trevelyan, *unemployed, of Epsom Downs, Epsom, Surrey.*

137 A Mother's Day message

Yvonne, the author's wife, writes: 'This prayer was written by my husband in the early hours of Mother's Day last year. He got up at 2 o'clock in the morning and cannot really remember writing it, but there it was in the morning. Our son was killed in his car three years ago on the island of Mallorca. He was 19 years old.'

To a wonderful spirit
To a wonderful Mum
I'd like to send thanks
From your only Son
I came to the earth plane
For a lesson to learn,
You taught me true love
and then I returned
I walk in your shadow
I'm with you always
I'll be there by your side
till the end of your days
And then we'll go forward
To the Heavens above
With all of our family
Seeking God's love.

To Mum
From your ever-loving Son
Jonathan

Robert Wood, *owner of restaurant and takeaway, Highcliffe on Sea, Christchurch, Dorset.*

138 A cry from the heart for the land and people of Northern Ireland

Our loving heavenly Father
come and be our Lord again
so that our hearts may burn.
Burning with a fire that will
not go out for thee. Make our
lives shine forth like stars
from the sky above showing
light to those who live in
darkness. How we are blessed
with all thy creation which
gives us hope for the future,

for a future without thee would
be very dark indeed. Thy
word tells us we are thy
children, children of a living
God and one day we will be
with you in glory where truth
liveth for ever. Amen.

Thomas Russell Elliott, *retired signwriter, of Old Cavehill Road, Belfast, Northern Ireland.*

139 Prayers before worship

God of all wisdom, you know who has come here and why.
In the way the music touches forgotten memories,
In the way the Bible shows us truth about ourselves,
Answer some of the needs here today, God of all wisdom.

God, when you speak the word,
Meaning comes out of chaos, darkness dissolves into light.
As we gather now, speak the word among us.
We need meaning.
We need light.

God of all moments, all the centuries,
You have given us this hour to spend in worship
Make it appear as this day and no other, unique and never to
    come again.
Make it fit with the rest of our days and with your eternal
    purposes.

The Revd Eric Locke, *of Selly Oak Methodist Church, Langleys Road, Selly Oak, Birmingham.*

140 The writer's prayer

Lord God, my life is one long list of deadlines
and I am struggling to get through with barely gap between –
Dear Lord, be there to occupy what little space there is.

And intermittently there are rejection slips;
curt letters: Sorry, but you do not fit our plan –
Dear Lord, may I find room in Yours.

And then again, the words count more and more
and I must rearrange them to create another view –
Dear Saviour, work with me, lend me Your light.

Time is one big mill-wheel, heaving round the day,
dredging up more debris to strew along my path:
Lord, save me from monotony and fix my gaze on You.

But when my hand stops writing, my fingers cramped and sore,
my mind goes on creating and nothing stops the flow –
Lord, help me learn to rest in You, Creator of all good.

You gave this gift when I was young and revelled in its power,
But now I'm so much older, it's out of my control –
Lord, You are my protection – teach me the way of truth.

I need to get the balance right, discerning what is right,
Seek quality not quantity, cultivate the seeds –
Lord, only You can be so close to know my deepest thoughts.

Now, as I contemplate each task, momentarily renewed,
Seek ideas for each assignment, assess the market share –
Lord, be my eyes, ears, inspiration; speak Your words into my heart.

Patricia Batstone, *freelance writer and local Methodist preacher, of Honiton, Devon.*

141 When I am gone...

Do not be sad when I am gone,
When my brief life on earth is done.
Weep not beside my burial quad –
There's only dust beneath the sod.

I shall have joined, in boundless space,
The souls from each and ev'ry race
And creed and colour known to man,
Who all have shed the human span.

I shall be one step nearer to
The God who shall all things renew;
Who shall, in His own time and way,
Co-join with all in endless day.

I shall be part of that vast plan
Which shall unite Heav'n, earth and man
In worlds that seem to never end;
Too vast a scheme to comprehend.

I shall be gone, and yet so near
To all that I, on earth, held dear:
A breath away, to wish you peace
And bid your frets and worries cease.

I shall be waiting, biding time,
Away from earth's minaceous clime,
Until the day, when we shall be
United for eternity.

William Walker, *of Halton, Lancaster.*

142 Enfold and influence me, Lord

Enfold and influence me, Lord
Help me curb my uncertainty.

Help me be mindful of you, Lord
That I may know your presence.

Inspire and humble me, Lord
That I may know your purpose.

Enter my heart, Lord
That I may do your will.

Guide and use me, Lord
That I may live aright.

Nancy Bartrum, *of Witney, Oxfordshire.*

143 Picturing God – a prayer of adoration

God,
You are
Without beginning or end,
Creator of the universe;
The source of life and love.
You have all power and authority,
All wisdom and knowledge.
You are unique in your holiness,
Set apart from those you have created
And yet you are seen ever present within your creation.
You are seen in the beauty of your creation;
In the golden blaze of a sunset,
In the delicate glory of the flowers.
You are felt in the gentle touch of a friend.
You are heard in the whisper of a breeze.
God,
You are
So awesome and mighty,
Yet gentle and kind;

Righteous and just,
Yet full of grace and mercy.
God,
You are
The Shepherd who leads and protects.
You are
The Saviour who surrendered himself
To redeem humankind.
You are
The Father who feeds and nurtures and loves,
Endlessly, completely, unconditionally.
God,
You are
Though far beyond human imagination
Personal and intimate in your revelation of yourself
To all who will acknowledge you. Amen.

Susan Matchett, *of Halesowen, West Midlands.*

144

We offer up our moments of disquiet as well as joy. The unspoken
sufferings which beset us as well as the manifest challenges of our
daily life. Rekindle in us the source of inner peace in the Spirit.

Peter Wright, *primary school teacher, of south-east London.*

145

Draw us, O Lord,
deeper into prayer,
deeper into You,
until the song of our hearts
is in tune with
the singing of the spheres,
which has been
Your voice across the universe
since before time began.

Draw us, O Lord,
Deeper into You. Amen.

Margaret Henman-Stott, *writer, of Gedling, Nottingham.*

146 A personal prayer of repentance

Lord God, You are my Father. You have shown me and taught me right from wrong, and I have let You down. I have done this... I have thought this... I have failed to do this... . I am sorry and seek Your forgiveness. I am not just word-sorry, I am heart-sorry and action-sorry. Direct me, I pray, for it is hard to make amends; even when I know what to do it is hard to do it.

I will resist the temptation to do nothing and I will fight other temptations, too, believing Jesus is with me. Strengthen my resolve. Fill me with Your Holy Spirit. I will set out now to live like a son or daughter of whom You can be proud, for that is my deepest desire. So help me, Father God. Amen.

Robin Carmichael, *of Brambope, Leeds.*

147

This prayer was written as a reaction to an evening's television viewing. It illustrates how, rather than being passive observers of screen violence, we can apply the need for peacemakers in our own lives.

Please Lord.

Please Lord make all the peable stop fighting. Sorry for telling lies and hitting my brother. Please help me stop shouting at my Mum and Dad. Thank you for makeing the world. Amen.

Edward Fillingham, *aged 6, of Oxfordshire.*

Katherine Polland, aged 15

148 The cyclist

I cycle through your Creation of fields of corn
and hay, where fragrant shrubs and bushes greet me
and I am inspired by your undoubted Presence.

How wonderful is the work of your Hand, the beauty
of your Intent.

May I be beautiful in your sight as your Creation
is to mine.

David Munroe, *unemployed, of Worthing, West Sussex.*

149 Sunlight

A shaft of sunlight,
Purple, green and gold,
Came through the window
As I knelt in prayer.
Dear Lord, this beauty
Speaks to me of you.
Purple, the robe that
Jesus humbly wore;
Gold, the treasure
Hidden in a field;
Green is for growth,
Creation with its joys.
O Father, grant my Lord's humility
And love, the treasure of the Kingdom, told,
May both be mine,
As in temporary life
I now grow old.

Edgar A. Garrett, *retired Anglican priest, of Chichester.*

150 Prayer of thanks

*This prayer has been recited by the author every morning for the past
50 years. He and his wife have been married for 65 years and feel that
they have truly been blessed.*

My God, I thank you for having preserved us during the night;
watch over and protect us, our relatives and friends during the
day. Help us to overcome our difficulties and temptations.

Guard and protect us in our work and driving, have care for
others and bring Peace to all nations.

Frank L. Payne, *retired dockyard supervisor, of Plymouth, Devon.*

151

Mother Mary, look upon
this child of helplessness, thy son;
let thy graceful spirit wander
all around it, over, under;
guard all others as thine own,
watch them through the life to come.

All their innocence divine
take for thyself, for it is thine;
all the evil that they know
belongs to us – what may we do
to foster in them thoughts of God,
to set their footsteps on the road
to righteousness and love of man,
to worship God, whose only Son
was once thine own, a son like them:
teach us to teach them so – Amen!

Robert Hey, *of Bury St Edmunds, Suffolk.*

Hidetoshi Tomikami, aged 15

152 Meditation with a newspaper

Lord of the days, and of the nights.

The guarantor of morning, and of morning's return.

I thank you for today's newspaper;
    my daily companion,
    my window on the world,
    my silent tutor.

I pray for those who write:
    may truth defeat bias
    may debate defeat bigotry.

I pray also for those who read:
    may intercession overcome curiosity
    may fairmindedness overcome prejudice

and may the Divine Light illumine us all.

So I meditate upon God, the newspaper and the reader.

Lord God, take these three, and fulfil the mystic potential of another trinity. Amen.

Revd Roger Haycraft, *of Hornchurch, Essex.*

153 A prayer when going into hospital

Lord, you are my shepherd,
I shall lack nothing.
You make me lie down on a hospital bed,
You lead me to the operating theatre
To restore my body.
You guide the hands of those who care for me,
For I am the apple of your eye.
Even though I walk through the valley of depression and pain
You are there with me.
You have prepared the way ahead.
You have given me friends who pray for me,
Anointing my head with oil as their prayers reach to you.
I know that nothing will happen to me that you have not planned.
All my days are spent in your presence,
Because you have promised never to leave me.
Amen.

Liz Piper, *housewife and student, of Liskeard, Cornwall.*

154 Grace

This is the author's supper prayer.

Dear Lord,
For every cup and plateful may we be truly grateful!
– Amen.

Mark Palmer, *gardener, of Deptford, south-east London.*

Lawrence Wong, aged 14

155 A prayer for help in coping with teenage girls

Dear Father of all,
After the teenage girls you've overseen
Please help me with mine,
'Such nice girls' they say, 'So sweet, so polite, so mature.'
Are we talking about the same people?
Amidst hairs in the sink, clothes briefly worn then scattered,
    telephones continually engaged with he saids and she saids,
    hair dye on the towels and worse
That 'What would you know?' look, 'You don't understand me'
and 'How can you be so stupid?' stance.
Making 'sorry' sound like a cuss
Sends me for the wooden spoon. Knowing that it's not the
    answer.
Please help me calm my rage. And laugh.
Help me be patient and wise.
Especially on days when I still feel an uncertain sixteen.

Help me remember what it feels like to be on the precipice of
    womanhood
And still want Teddy in bed at night.
Forgive me for nagging when one word will do.
Close down my mouth when I need to listen.
Forgive me for pushing what I think is a good idea.
Remind me every day that they are they, not me. We have
    different ways and talents. No worse, probably better.
Let me wonder at their beauty and loving souls.
But please have a little word on the quiet.
On my behalf.

Mrs Susan Chapman, *an occupational therapist and teacher, living in Dubai.*

Ellie Pang, aged 14

156 Broken wings

Lord, my faith has broken wings.
It can no longer fly up to your love
and praise you as it wants to do.
Bruised and battling against the wind,
the struggle has become too great for it.

Lord, pick me up in your loving hands
and shelter me –

and heal the broken wings of my faith.

Mary Hathaway, *of Nuneaton, Warwickshire.*

157

Grant to us, Lord, on this and every day,
Your peace and joy to guide us on our way;
Vision to see Your hand, O Lord, we pray,
In all our doings. May we always stay
In your control. Forgiveness, when we stray:
Wisdom to accept your plan, though days are grey:
And strength for problems – at your feet to lay
Our burdens: then your love our constant stay.
Grant these requests, we pray, O Lord, today.

Olwen France, *retired teacher, of Bury, Lancashire.*

158 First prayer of the day (discipleship)

Lord, please guide us through this day
In what we think and what we say,
And in ev'rything we do
Dear Lord, help us to follow you.

Grace Clarke, *lesson reader trainer, of north London.*

159 Turning fifty

I didn't want to be fifty, Lord.
The years had flown by so fast –
bringing up children, running the home,
keeping an eye on ageing parents,
earning money and taking well-earned holidays –
that suddenly, there it was:
My half century.

My eyes aren't what they were, Lord.
More wrinkles keep appearing all the time.
Sometimes I feel so tired.
I can't live life in the fast lane any more.
I wanted time to go backwards,
or at least to stay still for a while –
not to grow old.

But, now my birthday is behind me,
being over fifty isn't bad.
Thank you for the energetic years of my youth,
for the busy years of child-rearing.
Help me to be patient with my own body
and bless all the years that remain to me in your service.

Sue Minton, *wife/mother/teacher, of Rugby, Warwickshire.*

160

Let not my life's shadow,
Lord, eclipse your light
but let your power
roll away my sins,
as angels did the stone
at Easter light.

Sister Rosalie Burke, *of the Carmelite Monastery, Co. Dublin.*

161 Night prayer for sufferers

O God, have mercy this night on all those suffering agony of mind or body. Sustain them through the lonely hours of darkness when physical pain seems unendurable, sorrow is at its most harrowing and fears assume nightmare proportions. Lessen their discomfort, assuage their grief and instil into them new hope and courage. So that when dawn breaks they will have the resolution bravely to face another day.

Alison Barnes, *of Stansted, Essex.*

162 In a time of decision-making

Father, I am confused.

I have listened to well-meaning people
    who want to advise me
– but they don't agree with each other.

I have thought about the good points;
I have thought about the bad points;
I have thought about the people
    that my decision will affect.

I need your help – please –

Direct your Holy Spirit
    of truth and right-order
to be my guide through this quagmire
    of pros and cons.
Give me faith to trust you implicitly
    whatever the outcome;
and lead me safely along the path
    which I should tread.

Edna Eglinton, *retired secretary, of North Tawton, Devon.*

163 Prayer for an unborn child

Made in love, nurtured in love, surrounded by love, loving back without ulterior motive, you bring God to earth. May your life be blessed and a blessing to others. May your heart reflect the love you have received from God, from your parents, from us all. May you always be fulfilled and at peace and continue to be enfolded in love all the days of your life. Amen.

Frank Furlong, *of Berkhampstead, Hertfordshire.*

164 A prayer taught me by my grandmother

Dear Father whom I cannot see,
Smile down from Heaven on little me,
Let angels through the darkness spread
    their holy wings about my bed.
And keep me safe because I am
    the heavenly shepherd's little lamb,
Dear God and Father watch and keep
Mummy and Daddy while they sleep.
Teach me to do what I am told
    and help me to be as good as gold.

Ruth MacCabe, *retired, of Snodland, Kent.*

165 On losing a child

A child died,
I cried.
How could it be
This gift to me
Should be no more,
And my eyes so sore?

I struggle in vain
I'm still in pain.
Will I ever know
Why it should be so?
Lord, come to me now,
Before you I bow.

In God to trust
I find I must,
To find a way
Through my dismay,
And see God's hand
In all He planned.

Soul be at peace,
Mind, find release,
Heart, body, soul
Now be made whole,
I know you care;
Lord, hear my prayer. Amen.

Stanley Fitzsimmons, of *Sherwood, Nottingham.*

166 Prayer for today

Dear Lord, help me face without fear
    the challenges ahead today;
Guide my hand in working with others
    to be fair and just;
Direct my eyes to those with needs
    not self-evident;
Compassion in dealing with those
    less fortunate than me;
Insight to discern the needs of those
    whose cares are burdensome,
And lead me, Lord, to greater trust
    in fellow man when self-doubt sways my mind.

Peter W. Whippy, *communications manager, of Kraainem, Belgium.*

167 Funeral prayer

Dear Lord,
When death is upon him,
Place thy hands on his heart,
And draw his life into yours.
Help him to help himself,
And we will be yours always.
We will never leave his bedside,
Though we travel far and wide.
God bless his beginning and his end.
Amen.

Becky Mason, *aged 13, south-west London.*

168 The gift

Dear Lord, my love-Lord, my liebe-Lord,
how softly you come, bringing your gift,
sweet death.

I feel your breath upon my face,
I breathe your fragrance,
hear your song.

With your left arm you cradle my head.
With your right arm you embrace me.

You part the fibres of my being
With your loving fingers.
You unlace and discard the traces of age.
Into the spaces you breathe your own Spirit.
The essence of your Presence fills me.

My dear-Lord, my Love-Lord, my Liebe-Lord,
how lovely are your hands,
how gentle your caress,
how precious the kiss of your lips.

As you have loved me and lived me, Lord,
so die me.
Die me into Life with you forever.

Betty Haskell, *of Ackworth, West Yorkshire.*

169 A prayer for the hesitant

When I hesitate to say a prayer,
I think of those for whom I care.
Who will I ask to keep them well?
There's no one else my fears to tell.
Thank God they're happy, can work and play.
'Was that a prayer?' I heard you say.

Stan Murphy, *nurse manager, of Newton, Chester.*

170 Prayer for those departed

Father, we thank you for those whom we loved so much but see
no longer. In time the aching pain of their loss will lessen, but we
want the memories to live on so that they are still real to us. May
their example and their love for us be transformed into positive
good in our lives and actions. Keep us firm in the hope that we
shall all be reunited in Heaven. In your name, Amen.

Mary Rose de Lisle, *of Oakham, Leicestershire.*

171

Dear Lord,
Walk into my mind that I may think aright.
Come into my heart that I may experience
   your love and strength and learn to love others.
Strengthen my body so that it can be used in your service.
Make me a whole person so that you can dwell in me and I in you.
Amen.

Mrs Effie Dimmock, *of Wallington, Surrey.*

172 Eternal Father

Eternal Father,
Grant, we beseech thee,
The wisdom to use our ears, to perceive your word.
Our eyes, to see your light.
Our mouth, to taste the fruits of your earth.
Our hands, to touch and become one with your creation.
Our nose, to inhale the intoxicating delights of your nature.
Our compassion, that we may live for each other.
Our soul, that we may be ever closer, O Lord.
To the eternal glory of your name.
Amen.

Stephen R. Gee, *general sales manager, of Maldon, Essex.*

173 Beginnings

Be this unfamiliar work to me
The newness of your fresh creation.
Be the strangers I must meet today
The marvel of your incarnation.
With the laughter of your Spirit
Chase my anxiety and fear.
Mother, Maker, Saviour, Wisdom,
Send me out and keep me near.

Fay Sampson, *of Selly Oak, Birmingham.*

174 Why me, a grieving parent?

O Lord,
May grieving parents everywhere
   concentrate on what they do have and not
   on what they are missing.
See them through the dark times and
   guide them until they emerge triumphant
   into a brave new light.
Cure their melancholy, if not for a lifetime,
   a day; if not for a day, an hour.

Sweet compassionate Lord, console your
isolated hearts and grant peaceful lives to
they who whisper: 'Why me, a grieving parent?' Amen.

Christine Thouroude, *of Cambridge.*

175 The all-surpassing Spirit

Lord, you know I don't like praying.

It is the end of a busy day and there are still things to do at home
– the meal to prepare, the ironing, the washing – things crowding
in on my mind.

Yet, Lord, I feel compelled to kneel here before you. I don't know
what it is, but I must come to you.

I thank you Lord that there is a 'force' driving me to kneel here
before you. So as I come before you, I just ask that you will allow
this 'force' to intercede for me.

Thank you, Lord, that this is the Holy Spirit working in my life
and I ask, Lord, that it will always be so. That no matter what else
there is to do your Spirit will override everything else in my life.

Already I feel better.

Mrs Karen Corbett, *local government officer, of Southport, Lancashire.*

176 Evening – provision

Forgive me, Lord Jesus.
Thank You for being with me, for helping me.
You didn't take away the problem,
but You were with me in it.
I feel so humbled.
You came to me, not in rebuke, not in might or power,
but kneeling at my feet,
to serve me, You said,
to be available to me.
Now I know how the disciples felt
    when You washed their feet.
You so often surprise and humble me, Lord.
Thank You for being so magnificently unpredictable.
Thank You for loving me.

Sheila Bester, *of Swaffham, Norfolk.*

177 For a deserted friend

My friend's husband has left her, Lord
Help her in her distress
Help her in her humiliation
Help her see that life can still be good
May she be filled with the joy and peace of your love, Lord. Amen.

Margaret Loughran, *retired health visitor, of Headington, Oxford.*

178 I lift up my eyes

I lift up my eyes to the hills above
And down comes help to strengthen my heart.
Divine intervention from the God of Love
Who makes all things with his affectionate art.

He does not allow me to fall by the way –
His eyes are never closed in sleep.
He watches over me day by day
Just as He guards all His wandering sheep.

The green and the good things constantly strive
To render me hale and keep me alive.
Praise be to God and to Jesus his child
Who controls my outgoings and blesses my life.

Peter Gledhill, *retired clergyman, of Gwynedd, Wales.*

179 To the God of *No Name*

Hearken to my prayer, humans,
And Gods of the ancient world,
Listen to my words,
Heed my warning
And understand my plea.

Know that each night
I weep for the ills
    of this world.
And see all the pain,
    torture and murder
        that is carried on in the name of
        goodness, purity and honesty.

Hear my screams,
    divine children.
That die inside, empty,
    frustrated by the outside,
Unreceptive to the idea of unity
And cold to the process of compassion.

Now, what now,
In this lonely time you ride,
While hate fills the lines of light
And darkness hides in no shadows.
I pray for the eyes of man
    to open and witness reality.

I beg of humans to fault their own.
Forsake their ego.
This I pray for in no human's name
Nor in images of previous Gods
But in the idea of the selfless
In understanding
    love
    honesty
    respect
    tolerance
    and compassion
In the name of the One. Amen.

Esther Foreman, *student, of London.*

180 My prayer today

Fill my life with hope, dear Father
Let it be my prayer for today.
Fill my heart with love, dear Father
Let it be in all I do and say.
Fill the world with joy, dear Father
Let it be seen where I work and play.
Fill my soul with peace, dear Father
Let it never be taken away.

For the sake of my Lord and Saviour
Who died for me on the Cross that day,
Let your peace, love and joy, dear Father
Live and reign within my heart I pray. Amen.

Joan Stangroom, *retired, of Romford, Essex.*

181 In childlessness

Lord, help me change the nappy of the child I never bore. Let's
blow some kisses through her timeless hair, then smooth with
love the balding dandelion, then count the dimples on her starfish
hands, then gently squeeze her cheeks into a smile.

I see her crawling lonely on the shore. The upturned head bends
fleshy neck into the softest folds. Twice-dimpled elbows match
pneumatic knees. Upholstered feet make small prints in the
shifting sand. But as I run the vision fades away, declaring itself
to be a dream.

All things, O Lord, are possible for you. Hold tenderly the image
in your arms, this pulsing icon of a helpless world. Move me to
love the baby in the dying man, the dribbling infant in the
toothless tramp, the clumsy toddler in the old, arthritic nun.

Please hold her for me while I pray and smile her whole and feed
her with my dreams. Take her to a mirror; let her watch her cry.
Who knows when she may toddle there at will, bedimpled and
benappied, though set free? One day she'll stand there long
enough to love.

Louise Swanston, *religious sister of St Francis of Assisi RC Church, London.*

182 Dear Lord, accept the prayers we offer

This prayer can be sung to the tune of 'St Clement'. After writing it, the author was moved to become involved with the Christian Animal Welfare Movement.

Dear Lord, accept the prayers we offer,
For all Thy creatures in our care.
That none may suffer fear or violence,
Your guiding hand be always there.

For each and every humble sparrow,
Our Master marks their single fall,
Teach us to strive, and never weaken
The tireless fight to save them all.

Give us a heart of tender mercy,
Let no wild beast in suffering lie.
For them eternal freedom granted,
By hunters gun no more shall die.

Far round the world this prayer is offered
For strength and guidance from above,
Make us aware of all their suffering,
And keep them in Your wondrous love.

Linda J. Bodicoat, *of Earl Shilton, Leicestershire.*

183 A short prayer for today

Lord, may all those I have wronged
    know thy comfort.
May my sins be behind me,
May thy servant know thy peace.

John Philipson, *of Broadmoor, Berkshire.*

184 God our Creator and Saviour

Almighty God, our Creator, our Saviour, and our Guide through life, and at the end, our Judge. We worship you, and look for the coming of your Kingdom and wish to do your Will in all things. We thank you for our material benefits of all kinds. Please forgive our sins of all kinds, and teach us to forgive all those who offend us. We trust you to help us deal with all temptations, and to protect us from evil events and evil influences.

We rejoice that yours is the kingdom, the power and the glory for ever and ever. Amen.

Dr Noel Pratt, *of Norwich, Norfolk.*

185 A child's Easter prayer

Different seasons, different places;
Different customs, different races;
Easter eggs and smiling faces;
Please accept these our graces,
at Easter time around the world.

Glenys M. Philips, *part-time bank clerk, of West Glamorgan.*

186

The author wrote this in 1947 after the sorrow of losing her family in the Holocaust. At the time she was a nurse in the hospital attached to the School of Tropical Medicine in Liverpool, tending the wounds of soldiers who had been in the Far East.

O, God, please give me peace of mind
  and please give me tomorrow
  and make the world seem less unkind
  and soften our sorrow.

Edith Bown, *retired health visitor, of Maidstone, Kent.*

187 Noel

Lord of the universe
Source of creation
Angels adore
And the Heavens applaud.

Lord of the world
Embodied in Jesus
Embodied again
In the host and the wine.

Babe in my heart
Lover on Calvary
Lord of my being
And light of my life.

Dr Cormac Rigby, *Church of the Most Sacred Heart, Ruislip, Middlesex.*

188 Morning prayer

See page 140 for the full
version of this prayer.

189 Teach us, Lord

Teach us, Lord, to judge less and to understand more: that, by
accepting ourselves and one another, we may come to a deeper
understanding of you.

Mrs Robin Stemp, *of Cambridge.*

190 Dear Lord and Father

Dear Lord and Father of all life,
You have taught us not to fear death
   for our loved ones or for ourselves;
You have taught us that when we die
   we do not fall out of your loving care,
   and that death is not an end but a beginning;
You have taught us that unless we turn our backs on you
   and despise your promises,
   death is a new beginning on the way to eternal life with you.
Keep us strong in faith, dear Lord,
   especially when grief or self-regarding fear
   make it hard for us to believe;
For the sake of your Son, our Lord Jesus Christ,
   who died for us and rose again in glory. Amen.

Very Revd Murray Irvine, *of Ottery St Mary, Devon.*

191 Help!

Please God, Please Help!

Help me to want You to help me, to believe that You will, to
accept what You do, and to thank You. Amen.

Noreen Hare, *retired physiotherapist, of West Bridgford, Nottingham.*

192 Desire for God

My God, I yearn for you;
Assuage my hunger with your life-giving bread;
Quench my thirst from the well of your Spirit;
Refresh my weariness with the rest of your quiet;
Warm my coldness with your sacrificial fire;
Better my poverty with the riches of your grace;
Cover my nakedness with the clothing of your righteousness;
Satisfy my longing with the bliss of your love;
and at the last crown all my desiring with the joy of your
presence. Amen.

James Bogle, *of south-east London.*

193 A prayer for women who have lost their self-esteem

Dear Lord, help us to understand the difference between the
destructive sin of false pride and the calm blessing of self-esteem,
so that when we are depressed and all our efforts seem worthless,
we may remember that in you we have a special resource. Give us
grace, then, to go courageously into the world and use our God-
given talents to your glory. Amen.

Pat Laycock, *of Addingham, Ilkley.*

194 Alone

Lord Jesus,
Sometimes I feel that nobody knows
What I'm going through.
Nobody visits me or 'phones me
or writes to me.
It seems, sometimes, that days go by
I'm here alone, with nobody to talk to.
Help me to remember, in these times,
that
You are here and that I can talk to You,
Lord.
Don't leave me alone, Lord. Amen.

Michael Booth, *unemployed for four years,*
of Dewsbury, West Yorks.

Hugo Wheatley, aged 15

195 Gratitude

O God, we gratefully thank you for all kindness
from our fellow men and all beauty in nature and
the arts. Help us always to look first for these good
things, and not to dwell uselessly and resentfully on
evil and ugliness, but to think of them only when
we can help to remedy them.

Miss Alethea Hayter, *biographer and literary critic, of south-west London.*

196 Our Father

Our Father
    Who says there is a heaven,
    help us to keep your name holy
    on our lips.
May your rule in our lives
    be dominant
    and that first of all
    we find out
    what your will is,
    so we can do it
    as your will is done by
    angels and saints in heaven.
Give us this day
    all the resources
    we need to carry this through.
Forgive us when we fail you,
    as we refuse to hold it against others
    when they hurt us,
    deliberately or not.
And keep the tempter away from us –
    you know we're weak –
    delivering us and our loved ones
    from unadulterated evil.
For your kingdom
    is the only reality that matters,
    you are the ultimate source of life,
    and a glorious sight
    without end.
We say so too.

Ivy Hudson, *of High Shincliffe, Durham.*

197 For children

Dear Heavenly Father,
You have promised in your Word to fulfil
the desire of those who fear you. I reverence
you and worship you, and my deepest desire
is that my children and grandchildren
shall come to know and love you too.
Grant this for the sake of your Son,
Jesus Christ our Lord. Amen.

Elsie Tonge, *retired schoolteacher, of Heathfield, East Sussex.*

198 For employment

A prayer which was answered within one hour in 1962.

Lord, give me a job today.

Revd William Carrington Smith, *of Rochester, Kent.*

199 God's choice

The author began writing prayers for her daughters as they were growing up. This is the first to be published.

Being a boy or being a girl
Being a woman or a man
Is not our choice
But God's alone
We should not interfere.
Let us pray that we shall see
The light in which we are meant to be.

Being black or being white
Choose any colour you like
Skin is always natural
It always feels the same.
Only fools do not know this
Let us pray and we shall believe
That Mother Nature does not deceive.

I can be quite rich
I can be quite poor
But what matters most for sure
Is how full of life, how sweet, how funny
Not simply a case of how much money.
Let us pray and beg to serve
That we may receive our just deserve.

Jesus loved the great and small
They all listened when He spoke
His message was simply of love and truth
Of equality and fair play.
Two thousand years ago He lived
Let us pray and hear his story
It lives on in our hearts, His glory.

Let us find a place to pray
Calm and quiet, alone or in Church
Just closing our eyes to see...
That secret place inside ourselves
Which twinkles like a star.
Let us pray to God on High
The Father of the eternal sky.

Let us pray and look deep inside
Searching, with nothing to hide
The inner truth is like a guide
for those who trust and do not fear
For Mother Nature, She is here...
Let us learn these prayers to say
To help us through each night and day.

Alison Fayers-Kerr, *of Crazies Hill, Wargrave, Berkshire.*

200 Here I am

Here I am, Lord,
    Forgive me.
Here I am, Lord,
    Lead me.
Here I am, Lord,
    Show me.
Take my heart,
Take my mind.
Here I am, Lord.

Lilian Hodgson, *of Upton, Wirral.*

201 A prayer as we grow older

This prayer was inspired by, and is loosely based on, a prayer and an exhortation spoken by two men facing death in the Anglo-Saxon poem, The Battle of Maldon, which was composed by an unknown poet shortly after the battle in AD 991.

Eternal God, whose loving power is untouched by time,
May my thoughts be more truthful,
May my heart be more faithful,
And may my courage be greater,
As the years pass and my body grows weaker.
Thank you, Lord of Creation,
For all the joys I have known in this world.
I pray that when I have most need of you,
You will bless my spirit
So that it will journey in peace to your safe keeping
For ever and ever. Amen.

Patrick Nobes, *of Salisbury, Wiltshire.*

202 Silent scream

Loving Lord,   .
I'm in a strange mood.
A tumble of emotions.
Out of control.
And I don't like it.
There's massive frustration.
And it's growing.
I feel 'blocked'.
Silently screaming.

Touch me with insight,
to notice the roots of my pain.
Touch me with courage,
to be able to face into
all that has to be undergone.
Give me balance,
a sense of proportion,
and a conviction
that all, in the end,
shall be well.
Amen.

Fr Denis Blackledge SJ, *of Angmering, West Sussex.*

203 On my own

Lord, on my own I have no merit
    but with your presence I have your Spirit
You sent your Son that we could be one
    so not my will, but yours be done.

Lord, though we have our joys and sorrows
    we need not fear what will happen tomorrow
For today we have good news to tell
    if we trust in you, all will be well.

You help us daily from within
    to really fight that tempting sin
It is your word that sets us free
Yes, that does mean, even me!

Give us the will to go on searching
    and help us through the challenging journey
If we're close to you our struggles will ease
    and with your grace, we shall have peace. Amen.

Jill Conboy, *of Bath, Somerset. Mrs Conboy is florist and assistant lay chaplain at the Royal United Hospital, Bath.*

204 On receiving bad news

Lord, You know I've just received bad news
It's a blow, like a cold wind out of the East
I feel afraid
I can feel this sense of foreboding rising like an unwanted tide
I lose hope in the future when I start thinking about what I have heard
I feel alone
As if no one understands what I am feeling now
Lord, give me strength in this situation
Give me the gift of faith
Help me to be strong
Impress upon my spirit the fact that You love me
For the sake of myself
Impress upon my spirit the fact that You love me
That, in spite of everything, You are in control
Give me hope and a sense of purpose
Lord, I confess that I don't understand why this has happened
Help me to be honest with You about how I feel
Be my strength when mine has gone
Be my guide when tears hide the way

Make me strongest at my weakest point
Give me love when I feel anger or frustration
Impress upon my spirit that there is a purpose in all of this
Hug me day by day, Lord
Breathe on me, refresh me
I place the future in Your hands
Hold my hand and let us walk together through this
When You are with me I have nothing to fear.

Roy Etherton, *Tonbridge, Kent.*

205 Prayer in the morning

Dear Lord,
You know the innermost secrets
of my heart. Come into my mind this
morning and banish all unworthy thoughts.

Forgive my sins; cleanse and purify my
spirit; make me ready to receive your word
in the silence of the morning.

Give me the strength which I need for
this day's work, and sustain me through
the difficulties which I may face. Whatever
happens, help me to follow your example
of faith, courage and compassion, and
make me useful and good to those whom
I may meet today.

Bless my family and friends, and all
those I love, and those who love
me, through Jesus Christ our Lord. Amen.

Sheila Walker, *Tollesbury, Essex.*

206 For Alice

*This prayer was written after the author lost her daughter because of a
fatal genetic abnormality.*

An autumn child, a perfect dream
A happy chance, so it did seem.
Conceived when hope had long since passed
I knew this child would be my last.
And to my child I made a gift
Of love's commitment naught could lift.
But, like autumn leaves upon a tree,

Short lived the union was to be
Because, cruel master, Careless Fate
Was soon to change this glorious state.
My child was dealt a fatal blow
The reason why I'll never know.
Why make a life within my womb
Which has no future, only doom?
It seems a mystery to me
Although I've tried so hard to see
The purpose of a life so short
Humanity decrees you must abort.
But there's one thing that joins us still
And I know it always will
The chains of love wrapped 'round my heart
The strongest force won't prise apart.
And this love will not grow cold
For the child I couldn't hold
As she'll be kept in perfect grace
Until we meet, some time, some place
Where hopes and dreams can never die.
And so I pray to God on high
To keep her safe until the time
That I can claim this child of mine
And, when that moment comes be sure
Love will sustain for evermore.

Mrs Anne Griffin, *student, of Parkstone, Poole, Dorset.*

207 A prayer for today

Father, you know about all my yesterdays, the regrets, my griefs
and sorrows. Help me to look back with gratitude that you were
here.

Lord Jesus, I do not know what tomorrow holds and the future is
uncertain. Help me to place myself trustfully in your hands. Give
me the courage to keep moving forwards.

Holy Spirit, show me that it is today which matters. Whatever it
brings, give me the strength to be the person you want me to be,
and to live the life you want me to live.

For your name's sake. Amen.

Mrs Jane Gummer, *a housewife and the wife of an Anglican priest, of
West Ashling, Chichester, West Sussex.*

208 Jesus, let me

Jesus,
Let me understand, that I may be understood.
Let me be tolerant, that I may be tolerated.
Let me help, that I may be helped.
Let me forgive, that I may be forgiven.
Let me accept, that I may be accepted.
Let me trust, that I may be trusted.
Let me love, that I may be loved.
Let me know and accept my own truth.
Amen.

Kevin Whelan, *a writer, of Salthill, Galway, Ireland.*

209 Prayer for our leaders

Heavenly Father, I pray for the Prime Minister and his (or her) cabinet and members of the opposition parties. I pray for all in this nation who are in positions of authority and significant responsibility. I pray that they will conduct their lives with integrity and fulfil their duties effectively. Grant these men and women the ability to resolve problems and make wise, equitable decisions.

Father God, expose and root out those officials who are treacherous, morally corrupt or susceptible to bribery. Raise up and promote those individuals who are amenable to Godly counsel. Cause their opinions to be valued and their sphere of influence to increase.

Bless our leaders, Lord. Shield them from the effects of undue stress and overwork. Grant them good health and protect them from harm. Surround them with diligent, loyal and trustworthy colleagues.

I ask this in Jesus' name. Amen.

Carol Hind, *of south-east London.*

210 A prayer that an injured son will live

Dear Mother of God, my Mother and my
Advocate, I humbly ask that – as I
acknowledge your beloved Son to to be my Lord
and my God – you present my petitions
to Him.

I stand beside my injured son and abjectly
beg for his recovery. Grant him relief from his
physical suffering and escape from the confusion
and bewilderment as he fights his way back to
Sanity. Help me to accept with equanimity
the changes caused in my life by this disaster.
    Give me the courage to acknowledge my
helplessness to ease his pain. Let me know
the comfort of feeling your arm about my
shoulders. Let me not wallow in self-pity and
give me confidence to forge ahead, knowing that
my concerns are in your hands.
    I ask all this in the name of Jesus your
Son, who lives and reigns for ever and ever.
Amen.

Dr Elizabeth Hampson, *a recently retired casualty officer, of Richmond,
Yorkshire.*

211 Our ever-changing world

Lord, in a world of change
    We thank you for your changelessness.
In a world of doubt
    We thank you for your hope.
In a world of darkness
    We thank you for your light.
In a world of compromise
    We thank you for your Word.
In a world of haste
    We thank you for your calm.
In a world of noise
    We thank you for your peace.
Grant us your peace.
    Today and always. Amen.

Doris White, *of Wrexham, north Wales. Mrs White teaches at a junior
school in Wrexham, where she co-ordinates the religious education
curriculum. For several years she was involved in writing and
broadcasting on the daily religious slot on her local radio station.*

212 Find me, O Lord

Find me, O Lord, find me,
In all of Your Love, find me,
When I am lost and don't know what to do,
O Lord, find me.
Please call me, call my name,
I know I will hear You,
You have called me before.
Please find me, forever let me love You,
You have loved me with so much love,
Let me speak to You when I am afraid,
Hear me, O Lord, and love me. Amen.

Thank You, Holy Spirit of God, for Your Love.

Betty Baker, *a widow, of Shirehampton, Bristol.*

213 Jewels of life

Forgive me.
You give me the most beautiful, rare and precious stones for
my life's necklace. Reluctant to wear them and slow to give
them as love gifts to others, I discard or lose them.

Forgive me.
You give me the most pure, strong yet delicate chains on which
to thread the shining stones. But I neglect your silver and
your gold. I let it lie knotted and dusty in corners of old
jewellery boxes.

Forgive me.
Polish the stones and varnish them with your love.
Untangle the chains with your peace.

Amen.

Judi Marsh, *of Charlton Kings, Cheltenham, Gloucestershire.*

214 A prayer for recovered and recovering
alcoholics

Father, I thank you for doing what I found
impossible in my life. Through the power
of Jesus' death on the cross I have died
to alcoholism. Give me your grace to persevere
in my new life and to practise a relaxed
vigilance this day. I ask this in Jesus' name.

Revd Leslie Giddens, *of Hillingdon, Middlesex.*

215 In loss

This prayer is based on one of the prayers the author composed at various times for intercessions at St Mark's Church, Newnham, Cambridge.

O God of compassion, we commit to your love those who are mourning the loss of loved ones, and all who face loss of any sort, of health and strength, of mental powers, of home, employment or security, of hope, of love, of faith. Be with them in the darkness, Lord, and fill the emptiness with your love. For the sake of your dear Son Jesus Christ.

Betty Munday, *of Girton, Cambridge. Mrs Munday, a widow, is retired after a life as a headmaster's wife, magistrate, teacher and mother of two children.*

216 For the depressed

Dear Lord and Shepherd, some of those you love are low in spirits; depression blights their lives. Some have been abused, others are starving, lonely, grieving, deserted and supplanted. For all those who are downhearted, despairing and without hope we offer you our heartfelt prayers. You are an understanding listener, a supporting Saviour, friend and brother. Grant that the sufferers shall be relieved, the hungry fed, and the grieving comforted. Lift up the despondent heart, quieten the disturbed mind, and soothe the restless spirit, dear good Lord. Our prayers are urgent: make them equally effectual, as they are offered in your name.

Gwendoline Keevill, *of Brent Knoll, Somerset.*

217 Be close

The author wrote this prayer 20 years ago, when he was 18, and it has guided him through the years since.

Be close in your attachment,
Be bold in your resolution,
Be soft in your tongue,
Be sharp in your mind.
Have plenty of thought
    and
Be pure in knowledge.
Follow the world of wise men,
    and give no man your scorn.

Double your wheat store,
    and guard well your mind.
Attend to the following herd with love and caring,
Please the finality with dreams of non-violence.
Be avoided amongst changing circles,
Know the minds of men, far and near,
Peace is the deliverance of wisdom.
Follow the knowledge of forgetting,
Be clear in mind and spirit,
    and walk close to no stranger.

Be calm,
Be quiet,
Be in love with All.

Neil Smith, *of Arundel, West Sussex.*

218 A thanks for friendship

Dear God, thank you for making
it possible for him to choose to
be a friend to me, so giving me
the inspiration for a faith, for
hope and for happiness that I
never expected to feel.

Christine Cordey, *of Bradford
on Avon, Wiltshire.*

Ellie Pang, aged 14

219 A prayer for creation

This prayer was written by Fr McGreal after the rising waters of the Medway, attributed to global warming, threatened the medieval fabric of the Pilgrims' Hall at the world-famous Aylesford Priory, where he is sub-Prior.

Lord, in Your love You created our planet and made it a place of great wonder, power and beauty.

We, your servants, have not heeded the gentle balance of Your creation and through our selfishness we have caused hurt to Your creation.

Help us to heed the signs of our selfishness as seen in global warming and may we, even at this late moment, do all we can to heal our planet.

We beg Your help and protection in this work of love for Your creation.

We make this prayer through Your Son, the eternal Word who lived among us. Amen.

Wilfrid McGreal OCarm, *of Aylesford, Kent.*

220 Mid-life crisis prayer

Dear Lord, the children are gone
I feel a bit old
My bills are not small
My mind is not sharp any more.
I am not more smart
My life is half past
Over the hill I am, fast.
But Lord, You are still with me
I will live with You eternally
In Heaven all things are free.
I have more insight and
maybe I am more wise.
Every morning my life is anew and
in the end, I will at last be with You. Amen.

Rafael Deogracias, *translator and interpreter, of Perry Barr, Birmingham.*

221 A teacher's prayer

The author wrote this at the Roman Catholic Salesian retreat centre for young people at Savio House in Bollington near Macclesfield, where he had been on retreat with a small group of teachers and pupils from the Painsley RC High School in Cheadle, Staffordshire.

May I always see you, O Lord, in the pupils that I teach.
May I learn to respect them as persons with their own point of view.
May they – and may I – grow in awareness of the fact that we all need each other and that we all need you. Amen.

Piers L. A. James, *of Cheadle, Stoke-on-Trent.*

222 O Man

O Man, who was manna,
Poured down from Heav'n
Into my vast, bleak wilderness,
The desert of my soul,
I hunger, feed me.

O Water of Life,
Who baptised me in the river
Which poured from your side
To water the desert,
I thirst, quench me.

O Blood that was let
To relieve my pain,
Poured on the darkness of my soil
To nourish your seed there,
I wilt, strengthen me.

O Lamb that was led out
To graze on the hill,
And paused in the bitter pasture
As our Passover feast,
I'm lost, lead me.

O Love, who pours in
In the midst of my pain,
To comfort and sustain me
When I fall in the dark,
I hurt, hold me.

D. Bentley, *of Newcastle-upon-Tyne.*

223 Prayer for Arnaud de Contades

The author was spending a weekend at a château in France, during
which the owner's first grandson was born. 'Priez pour le petit Arnaud,'
he was asked, and this prayer was the result.

I could have asked for grace that he might live
With all that Nature, all that Art can give.
With every noble virtue which we find
Enrich the soul or ornament the mind;
Of God's abundant treasury aware,
Eager to taste and generous to share;
Ready for pastures new when times move fast,
Yet always mindful of the cherished past;
That in each chosen walk he might pursue
Whate'er is Good and Beautiful and True,
Nor yet disdain, engrossed in worldly strife,
The saner pleasures of a simple life.
My faith forbids. It is not in my creed
To tell my Maker what he knows we need.
These may be pearls which we must sacrifice
To gain that one true Pearl of costly price.
So grant him, Lord, that only gift divine
Which turns life's water into purest wine:
Thy richest, dearest blessing from above,
His God, his neighbour and himself to love.

Canon Ian Dunlop, *former Chancellor at Salisbury Cathedral, of The*
Glebe, Selkirk.

224 Know that I believe

Dear God,
Whoever, whatever and wherever you are, know that I believe
you exist, that you are aware of me, irrespective of any label I
may choose to attach to my belief, and that you will always hear
my prayers, however I may communicate them and wherever I
may be. In recognition of these things, and in so far as it pleases
you, do for me always what I now ask:

Teach me to see that I need to know and understand myself
wholly before I can be of real help to others.

Guide me to recognise and accept differences between myself
and others and help me to live with them as tolerantly as
possible.

Remind me that it is what I do for others, wherever possible unseen, unheard of, unselfishly, and for their own sake, that matters most.

Direct me to speak out and uphold timeless values, founded on our forebears' experience, and to resist change for change's sake.

Give me the depth of perception to know when to stand and fight and when to give way, so that goodness may prevail in all things.

Develop in me the wisdom to apply the essence of your wishes sensibly to all that I am exposed to in the times in which I live.

Sharpen my ability to balance the idea of free will with its myriad limitations borne of others and the environment.

Keep my mind open to all that goes on around me so that I may identify from what happens that which will ever increase my insight.

Enthuse me to lead by my own example so that others, by their own choice, may be inspired in good ways and do likewise.

Make me realise that redemption and forgiveness are yours alone to grant and that these can only be truly earned by deeds, not words.

Allow me to represent myself when I can, to receive a fair hearing, and to prevent others usurping my person, in all matters.

Thank you, God. Amen.

Kalvin Haley, *Army officer, of Chelsfield Village, Kent.*

225 Hymn of praise

For laughter we praise you, O God,
    And all the release that it brings:
It makes us to rise up with joy,
    And smile at the difficult things;
It helps us to look at ourselves,
    And face up to life with its strains,
To carry on living each day,
    And even to suffer our pains.

For singing we praise you, O God,
    And all the rejoicing it brings:
In filling our lives with delight
    It deepens the meaning of things;

Our sorrows are turned into joy;
   We're given new strength for the strife,
And find we are thirsting again
   To drink from the fountain of life.

For worship we praise you, O God,
   And all the renewal it brings:
It lifts up our soul from the earth
   To apprehend heavenly things;
It speaks to our hearts of your love
   And beauty surpassing all thought;
It shows us your glory afresh
   In all you have patiently wrought.

Revd Allan Bowers, *of Sidmouth, Devon.*

226 O Jesus Christ my Saviour

This prayer was sung by the author at her adult baptism.

O Jesus Christ my Saviour
I come to you at last.
This is my new beginning
Forgive me now my past.
I can hide nothing from you
You know just how I feel.
O cleanse my heart and soul, Lord
As humbly, here I kneel.

O Jesus Christ my Saviour
We're kneeling side by side.
I'm promising to follow
You've promised me to guide.
There is no other way, Lord,
That I can perceive.
To show how much I need you,
Lord Jesus, I Believe.

Mrs Jeanne Bailey, *a national insurance inspector with the Civil Service, of Forest Hill, south-east London.*

227 The God who disturbs

The author wrote this in March 1994 at a time when she was struggling to understand what her faith said in terms of the problems in the world around her. She writes: 'At about that time, the BNP were active in Millwall and I was challenged by the fact that, while my non-Christian friends were active in organisations to combat racism and other injustices, I, a Christian, was doing very little.'

Praise to God who disturbs us in our complacency,
Who makes us dissatisfied with our lives because
    they are not as He would have them be.

Praise to God who shows us the wrong that we must put right,
Who makes us angry when we see evil and ashamed when
    we turn away and do nothing.

Praise to God who has shown us the way to live,
Who challenges us to live out His love in this world,
    in the midst of fear, pain and hatred.

Praise to God who gives us His power.
Disturb us now with your love.
Show us what we must do.
Turn our dissatisfaction, our anger and our shame
    into loving action,
And Your will be done on earth, as it is in Heaven.
Amen.

Carolyn Lawrance, *of Woodford Green, Essex.*

228 Thank you for holding me

This prayer was written for a family service at the author's village church.

Heavenly Father,
thank you for holding me
when the world lets me down
for loving me when I feel unlovely
– help me to reflect that love.

Thank you for being my light
in a dark world, where sometimes
I walk as a stranger
for shining and never going out
– please let me shine too.

Heavenly Father,
thank you for being a friend
who never leaves me, who is
always faithful even when
I fail you
– teach me to be a good friend.

Thank you for carrying my worries
for knowing that tomorrow
is in your hands for a purpose
– strengthen my trust in you.

Heavenly Father,
thank you that in a fast, uncertain
world, you remain the same forever
always constant, always true
– help me to grow closer to you.

In Jesus' name I pray. Amen.

Mrs Helen Clarke, *of Great Wilbraham, Cambridge.*

229

O my Lord and my God, I love you with all my heart.
All I have comes from you
All I do I offer to you.

Please help me to remember that you love us all so that
I despise neither myself nor others but become a reflection
of that love.

Please guide us and keep us safe.

Mrs Mary Green, *of Seaford, East Sussex.*

230 Relationships

O God, let my relationships with
   my fellows be those of intercession,
   of love,
   and of service.

Norman Kirby, *of Wembley, Middlesex.*

231 What will I say when I meet You?

*The author and his wife, both in their mid-seventies, are Lancastrians
who have lived in Northern Ireland for 41 years. From childhood, he
was brought up in the Church of England, and she in the Baptist church,
but they pray now with the Presbyterians. This prayer was selected from
a large collection which he wrote as a solace when his wife, Ruth, was
close to death. The prayer was born also of doubts, fears, introspection
and a liking for words and rhythm.*

What will I say when I meet You, my Saviour?
How do I tell You the things that I did?
How to account for the sins I committed,
Not what You told me and not what You bid?

What will You say when I meet You, my Saviour?
Will You recount the long list of my sin?
Will You forgive all my sins and omission,
Forgive all my loved ones and those of my kin.

What will You say when we meet in Your Heaven?
I'll ask You to bless me, forgive and to heal,
Humble and penitent, full of contrition,
Cleanse me of sin as before You I kneel.

Harry Wakelin, *of Bangor, Co. Down, N Ireland.*

232 Forgiveness

O God – forgiveness – what a word
it's quite impossible
How can I pray while full of hurt?
I can't, no good at all.
What is this thought that's crept right in ...
'don't believe I want to ...'
there now, that's really honest,
have I shocked even You?
May I still talk with You, O Lord –
well isn't that what praying is?
I do want conversation, Lord
so an answer would be nice ...
it's two-way communication
please God do answer me.
What? Oooh that's hardly fair;
but You are God and it's Your job ...
all right, now I can see
yes, You have forgiven me
so who am I to shout and cry
I can't forgive – no, no,
No, not alone I can't, that's right
so now I'll ask for help –
Please will You help and hold my hand
and hold at bay my pain
No, better yet, please take away
the angry thoughts still rife
and in their place please would You fill
yes fill me with Your love
leaving no place for hate to grow.
Then keep reminding me
that following in Your footsteps means
forgiving as You do.
What's that? Not just once You say
but seventy times seven
and even more may need to be ...
Let me get through once first!
O God – forgiveness – what a word
did seem impossible
but now thanks to You not quite,
not easy either but
possible at least; stay with me
Lord, help me see it through.

R. Fiona Fuhrman, *of Lewes, East Sussex.*

.33 Dear God, my God

The author, aged 94, describes herself as a lyricist who talks to God many times each day, and therefore finds it natural to pray. A friend told her The Times *was seeking prayers. 'He who hesitates is lost,' she wrote.*

Dear God, my God
From the beginning, to the ending of each day,
Be close to me,
Let me feel your presence.
So shall loneliness be dispelled,
Love and warmth prevail,
Love, the source of life,
The mind, the soul.

Dear God, my God
So freely do you give your love
To each and every one.
So we may pray and thank you God
For your forgiveness, and everlasting love.
When we fail your dear presence is
        still with us
At the beginning and the ending of each day.

Madeline Chase, *of Worthing.*

234 O Lord

O Lord,

Where there is an opening
let there be Light

Where there is a closed door
help me to open it

Where the door will not open
help me to knock

When the knocking is not heard
Let there always be your
glorious hope

In the name of Christ.
Amen.

Mrs Marian Masters, *an orthoptist, of Walsall, West Midlands.*

235 Two-fold prayer

The author says she lives on the strength of her constant 'hot line' to God.

All those of us who possess common sense
  Know that life isn't planned to be 'fair'.
Some sail along with no problems at all –
  While others have more than their share.
But problems are challenges we have to face...
  If only we knew the right way.
The answer is simple – we share them with God
  As we reach for His hand when we pray.

Lord, my prayer is two-fold: I seek comfort and hope for all
who are suffering in any way... and the courage to face the
challenge of my own handicaps and heartaches... secure in the
awareness of your presence and never-failing strength.

Joy Johnson, *of Tring, Hertfordshire.*

Jimmy Hung Hing Leung, aged 15

236 A prayer for goodness

Dear Father, please let these qualities grow in me:

Endurance, that I may be able to cope with the
position in life where you have placed me,

Fortitude, that I may have courage and constancy
in the pursuit of good,

Patience, that your love may shine through me,

Perseverence, to keep trying to climb the
hill 'difficulty',

Magnanimity, that I might be forgiving, and
free from resentment,

Wisdom, to seek the truth and have sound
judgement,

Through Jesus Christ our Lord. Amen.

Margaret Parbury, *of Widcombe, Bath, Somerset.*

237 No pretending

Lord, help me to come before you openly,
    not trying always to pretend that everything is OK.
You know when I've had a bad day, like today for instance.
I tried to put on a brave face with my family,
    pretending I was fine, because I didn't want them to suffer.
I wanted to scream and shout and let out my frustration,
    and I still do.
Lord, I don't want to take it out on you either,
    but I know you do recognise how I feel.
I know you won't be able to help me
    if I hide in a falsely cheerful exhortation,
    so give me the words to tell it like it is.
I need to tell you how I feel right now,
    so that I can cope with the times
    when everything goes wrong
    in a much better fashion.
Lord, help me to get my peace from you,
    the peace that passes all understanding
    but is comforting and available to those who ask for it.
Lord, I ask for that peace now, please. Thank you.
Amen.

Peter Comaish, *of Mill Hill, north-west London.*

238 Cassie's prayer

Someone up there knows us, as he watches from above
He sends us strength to help us, with buckets full of love.
We all have days of sadness, when skies are dark and drear,
But He is there to guide us, and rid us of our fear.
His love is never ending, for he has a special gift,
Of care and understanding, which gives us all a lift.
Our lives today are faster, the days pass by in haste,
We seldom stop to think of Him, His salvation, and His grace.
Lord, when we are young and foolish, please watch us from above,
Guide us toward the best things, your goodness, strength and love.
Then when we find we cannot cope, with our troubles and our strife,
Your powerful might, and all our hope, will last us all our life.

Cassie Buckley-Smallwood, *a retired secretary, from Victoria, Australia.*

239 Circle me

Circle me, Lord
 With the sacrifice of your Cross
  by which I am redeemed.
Circle me with the love that took
  you there.
Circle me always with the
  Power of the Holy Spirit
 Who raised you to Life
  and enables me to live for you.

Mrs Sybil Philp, *of Tring, Hertfordshire.*

240 Faith

Dear Lord,
Keep me ever mindful of your love and
compassion to help me through each day.
To have faith that you are always there to guide and
comfort me, so when evening comes and I lay down
to rest it will be with the knowledge that what I
have done and said will be worthy of your calling
and I can look forward to tomorrow with a light
heart and greater confidence.
And that, with You, faith is all powerful and the answer to all my
fears.

Marian Rawlinson, *of Sale, Cheshire.*

41 A builder's prayer

The author studied construction and was employed in the building industry as an estimator for 16 years. He recently left the industry to study theology at Leeds University, but says that construction will always be in his mind.

Almighty God, our Heavenly Father, Maker of all things,
Whose Son our Lord Jesus Christ was a carpenter in Nazareth:
Grant that the structure of our lives may be founded on the
    knowledge of your love;
That the fabric of our faith may be proof against all elements;
And that the windows of our hearts may let in your light,
    And show forth your glory to the world.
This we ask through the same, your Son, our Saviour, Jesus Christ.
    Amen.

Paul Gill, *of Adel, Leeds.*

242 A Sunday morning prayer for preachers

Almighty God, whose Word became flesh in your Son Jesus Christ, we commend into your loving care all those whom you have called to preach today, Sunday.

Forgive us when we forget that this is a calling and not a performance, that you alone have set us before your people with your Word in heart and mind.

Forgive us when we are tempted to entertain rather than to entreat. Heartfelt laughter from an at-ease congregation is therapeutic so let it be used to heal bruised spirits and to bring men and women to know you for themselves.

Thank you for those Sundays when we have known that we are off-form but you have used our preaching to speak to those whom you have known to be in deepest need, those who are there for the first time and those who are coping with burdensome doubts.

We pray for those who will be preaching, knowing that within the congregation are those who are undermining their ministry. Help them to resist the temptation to get back at them publicly and to be fully focused on preaching Jesus Christ and Him crucified.

We pray for those who feel burnt out. Lord, save them from chasing after being original, equip them with the infinite resources of Scripture.

We commend into your keeping those for whom preaching today is a blessed relief. The week is so full of everything to which they were not called. Bless them, Lord. Amen.

Revd Victor Sumner, *former secretary of the Baptist Ministers' Fellowship, of Ferring, Worthing.*

243 Thanksgiving for uncomfortable reminders

Father, we thank you for uncomfortable reminders that our commitment to You may not be as wholehearted as You yearn for it to be.

We thank You that these reminders may be found all around us, in books, through the media, in meeting people, in obituaries of men and women who have lived dangerously in Your service.

We give You thanks for Your servants who have spoken the truth at great cost; those who have been lone voices protesting against abuses; those forgiving bitter injuries; those living out a pattern of service, modesty and loveliness; those exemplifying the Beatitudes – the most uncomfortable reminders of all.

We praise you that reminders may come like lightning illuminating areas we might prefer to ignore.

Set beside these examples, we realise that we are too easily discouraged; that we sometimes grow careless of the rights of others; that we have deviated from the truth out of cowardice, indifference or selfishness; that our view has become narrow and our expectations circumscribed.

We thank You that the inspiration of Christlike people may stir us to repent and learn to live more abundantly. Like the prodigal son may we come ourselves and resolve to return to You, our Father, for forgiveness and a new life, surrendering all our being into Your service, acknowledging that we can also draw on the power which raised Christ from the dead, the power that is made perfect in our weakness.
Amen.

Elizabeth Hamilton-Jones, *of Cranleigh, Surrey.*

244 On the death of a son

This prayer was written by the late Gertrude Shillito, wife of a canon of the Church of England, on the death of her son, IV Lancelot Shillito, aged 34, who caught an incurable illness on holiday in Italy.

Grant that his life may enfold itself in Thy sight and find sweet employment in the spacious fields of eternity. Tell him, Gracious Lord, if it may be, how much I love him and long to see him again and if there be ways in which he can come, grant me a sense of his presence. Pardon, Gracious Lord and Father, whatever is amiss in my prayer and let Thy will be done.
My will is blind and erring but thine is able to do abundantly above all that we deserve.

Submitted by the author's son-in-law James Brown, *of Lymington, Hampshire.*

245 Jesus is beside me

My days are all enchanted
God is there to love
Jesus is beside me
Angels are above.

Who would be alone to die
With no one there to care?
Jesus is beside me
I can have no fear.

Gillian Sinclair Hogg, *poet and sculptor, of Newbury, Berkshire.*

246 A writer's prayer

We praise God that in the beginning was the word;
    that by his Word we are created and sustained;
    and that in Jesus, God has spoken his last word.
We praise God for the beauty and the power of words;
    for the joy of writing and the pleasure of reading;
    for the power of literature to inspire and challenge,
        to comfort and refresh,
        to make us laugh and to make us weep.
Grant us, Lord, minds quick to detect falsehood and sham,
    eager to follow truth.
Give us hearts to love, admire and praise what is good;
    and through our writing deepen our sympathy with all mankind;
    through Jesus, the Word of God.

Revd Simon Baynes, *Vicar of Winkfield and Cranbourne, of Winkfield, Windsor.*

247 Lord, you commanded us

Lord, you commanded us to love you and our neighbours as ourselves. You showed us how to love when you died for us on the Cross. You showed us how to do the Father's will. Grant, Lord, to each one of us this day, and all our days, the courage and strength to keep your commandments of love and to do the Father's will, on earth as in heaven, whatever the costs and whatever the consequences and, at the last, to rise with you to everlasting life and love. Amen.

Ian Blackshaw, *international lawyer, of Eversley, Hampshire.*

248 A private family prayer

Lord Jesus Christ, thank you for the many
benefits which my wife and I have enjoyed
in our lives.
   I pray that similar benefits may be enjoyed
by our children and grandchildren.
   I pray also that the souls of those of my
family who have died may rest in peace.
   Finally, O Lord, help me to accept death,
loss and disappointment as straws upon the
tide of life, and help me to seek continually
for that peace which passeth all understanding. Amen.

Hilary Eccles-Williams CBE, *of Solihull, West Midlands.*

249 Jesus, come alive

This prayer was inspired by Matthew 14:24–33.

Jesus, come alive for us
Let any captives free
We need your loving touch
So that we may live for thee.

At times we may be plagued with fears
Some real, some of our surroundings
But you can always
See through our tears
When we call out to you, Lord
You give us understanding.

'I will be there for you
Hold on to me
And as I fold my arms around you
I will accept and love you
      as part of me.'

Mrs Veronica Hartley, *a rail operator, of Southport.*

250 A brief morning prayer

Dear Loving Father, take this day
And make it yours in every way.
In all I think and say and do
Dear Saviour keep me close to You.
In those I meet help me to see

On every face a sign of Thee.
And as I work, Guide Thou my hand
That I may learn and understand.
Keep me from fear and grant me, Lord,
The gentle touch, the kindly word.
And where my thoughts and actions fail
There let Thy love and strength prevail.

Edda Hanington, *a retired doctor, of Brighton.*

251 God's answering machine

O Lord, I keep on trying
But you are never there.
I try to leave a word
To show you that I care.

I listen for the tones
And speak in careful measure
To ask for but a crumb
From your abundant treasure.

When you are never in
I don't know what to say
Because you know, my Lord,
how hard it is to pray.

I struggle to begin
And hesitate to utter.
So, likely, what you get
Is just some garbled mutter.

I try to bring myself
To say some words of sorrow,
But once again I fail –
I'll try again tomorrow.

So, Lord, leave me a message,
I don't care what you say.
Just leave a little sign to show
You hear me when I pray.

Frank Keetley, *a retired lecturer, of
Maltby, Rotherham.*

Ellie Pang, aged 14

252

The author describes this as more a 'stream of consciousness' than a prayer, but explains that this is how he talks to God.

Lord, I pray for Faith
I believe You are there.
I believe You love and care for me.
Help my unbelief. Show yourself to me.
Help me to see you in the people I meet every day.
   In the teacher. My daughter is a teacher and she tries to show something of your love to the children.
   In the doctor. I have a caring, conscientious doctor who is thorough and kind.
   In my neighbour. She is always ready to help me to tackle the simple difficulties of life.
   In my family. They love and care for me and my wife not out of gratitude or duty but because they want to.
   In my friends.
   In the people I meet in the pub, in the village tearoom.
   In the innumerable gifts of kindness I meet with every day.
Help me to see You in the life, death and resurrection of my Lord Jesus Christ.

He faced life with a cheerful and buoyant spirit.
He never saw want without turning aside to help.
He was insulted and reviled but did not turn on his persecutors.
He was kind and loving to his friends and his enemies alike.

Help me to see You in my need for You.

I know my life is incomplete. I don't just imagine that I have a need for You. It is You who has given me this restless and unsatisfied spirit. It is a need that only You can satisfy.

And when You have given me these glimpses of Your divine nature, help me, O God, to use them, help me to become more like You, more Christlike.

Help me to hallow Your name.

Tom Rees Jones, a retired industrial chemist and councillor, of Draycott, Derby. The author has for a long time been involved with his local church and has recently been confirmed an Anglican.

253 A prayer to the Spirit

O Great Spirit,
You are One and everyone
Perfect and perfecting
Clean and cleansing.

I wander this world
Like a child's balloon,
Tossed by the slightest breeze,
Buffeted by every raindrop;
Only dimly aware of that fine thread
Which anchors me and will not see me lost;
Still less aware of the unseen guiding hand
Of the child who holds that thread;
Less conscious still of the loving parent
Who leads that child safely home.

Loving Spirit,
Knowing at least that I know so little
I seek each day to still my restless mind
So that I might feel
The gentle pull of Your perfect will,
And I ask this one thing:

If it be for my highest good,
And for the highest good of all life everywhere,
Let me take, this day, one step closer
To fulfilling my life's purpose
As I understand it,
Or one step closer to understanding.

John Andrew, *of New Farnley, Leeds.*

254 A brief prayer of comfort

Lord Jesus, by your Spirit's grace
May I the Father's will embrace.

Fr Andrew Ryder, *a Roman Catholic priest from Rome, who helped out at St Catherine's Church in Lowton in the Liverpool archdiocese during the summer of 1996.*

255 A prayer for gardeners

Lord of all creation, breathe hope into my heart as I
approach each task.
Be in my fingers as I sow the seed, and dwell in the
soil at germination time.
Come with the rain which nurtures new growth and
Your Presence shine in the warmth of the sun.
And, when the plants and flowers reach their maturity,
I pray that You will grant me the vision to recognise
Your Eternal Glory.

Mrs Pauline Heathcote, *retired, of Lowdham, Nottingham.*

256 A thanks for life's blessings

Dear Jesus,
Thank you for blessing
me in every single way.
Thank you for guiding
me on every single day.
The years that you
have led me, through strife
and toil,
have prepared me for a
bright tomorrow.
In Heaven I look forward
to time with you,
my soul perfected and
spirit unrejected.
Please help me through
the remainder of this life,
and help me to love you
more and more. Amen.

Paul Gainsford Bailey, *a writer, of Cockfosters, Barnet, Hertfordshire.*

257 And we would not

The author wrote this prayer after a friend took her own life.

But, Father, we were only talking to her an hour ago! She seemed
quite all right then. We'd no idea that she was so near to the end
of her tether; why, she'd asked us to post her subscription to the
National Trust.

..hat more could we have done? We had tried to be good
.eighbours, without being too inquisitive. But she soon seemed to
get tired of people, and let them know it. She was always worried
about her health, thought she'd got the big C – but the doctor said
there was nothing really the matter with her. She was a great
worrier.

It wasn't as if she was hard up, after all. She wasn't out of work
with a family to care for. She had worked for a year or two when
she was young, but she never really needed to. What went wrong,
Lord?

When we're young, Heaven lies about us. We are a little world
made cunningly, with a whole universe in our heads. We know
the difference between right and wrong; we can lie on our backs,
put our toes into our mouths and be wrapped in a great cocoon of
love.

But nature pushes us out, out into the wide world we've made.
Well, You have made, and we have messed up. All manner of
things prey on us; the greed of those who couldn't care less about
destroying people with drugs or hate or bigotry. Are you
surprised we don't take a paper any more? There's never any
good news in them these days.

But what about your good news, Lord? Why doesn't that still
move us, mean more to us?

You wrap us in a great cocoon of love and forgiveness, if only we
will trust you. Help us to long for you, Father, as we long for
worth and security and peace.

Revd John Ticehurst, *URC minister, of Braunton, North Devon.*

258 A prayer of submission

Dearest Lord God,
  I love thee and worship thee.
  Thou art my guide, my comforter, my friend,
  My strength, my refuge, my rock,
  My life, my love.
  Without thee I am as nothing.
  Show me the life thou would'st have me lead,
  Thy will be done through me. Amen.

Michael Bradstock, *retired, of Clunas, Nairn.*

259 Listening to You

Give me listening ears tuned to only You
To know when You are talking to me
Ears ready to hear from You.
Give me a listening heart
A quiet heart ever conscious of You
A heart ever meditating on Your goodness
A heart full of praise for You
Give me a listening heart, Lord
Always open to You.

Mrs Dolapo Grillo, *a research assistant, of Barons Court, west London.*

260 We come to you

Our Father in Heaven,
We come to you in our emptiness, and ask you to fill us –
Fill us with your love and grace, by your Holy Spirit.

We come in our weakness, and ask you to make us strong –
Make us strong to stand for what is right
And to withstand the evil in this world.

We come in our poverty and ask you to make us rich –
Make us rich in the gifts of the spirit:
Love, Joy, Peace, Patience and Kindness.

We come in our loneliness –
May we know you as our friend and companion,
We come with our troubles and pains –
Meet our need for healing in mind and body, we pray.

Teach us, dear Lord, to come to you
As children come to loving mothers and fathers,
In complete trust, in simple love, with glad hearts,
For we come in the name of your dear Son, our Saviour,
Jesus Christ our Lord. Amen.

Eric Leat, *of Bookham, Surrey.*

261 A prayer for the sick

Merciful Lord, give comfort and healing to all who are ill, all who
mourn, all who are lonely, all who are afraid, all who feel dread in
their heart as each new day dawns and those who fear the long,
dark night. In your mercy ease their pain, calm their fears and
turn their despair to hope. When the lamp of their faith burns

low, rekindle the flame, create in them an inner serenity that
knows the comfort of Your presence and the absolute conviction
that nothing can separate them from Your love.

Elaine Robertson, *a church verger at St Wilfrid's Parish Church, of
Calverley, Pudsey, West Yorkshire.*

262 A dancer's prayer

Love, faith and hope
Are integral parts
Of the total person
And when they seem to be lost
They are only maybe blotted out
As the sun behind a cloud.

But the real hurdle to eternal life,
Apart from death itself,
Is forgiveness from God.
Please grant this to us
Where repentance is true.

Whatever ways we try to toe the line
I beg you God to accept and use
The life-spring or creation
That many of us contain
And which for some
Can only be expressed
Through the body in dance.
Thank you, God.

Janet Logan, *a dance teacher, hillwalker and former ballet mistress in*
Carousel.

263 When things are too much

Lord, when things get too much for me,
When I don't know which way to turn,
Comfort me, Lord, be close to me,
Help me know you care and are really there.
My friends don't always know what to say
    or do,
But you created all things,
You created me.

I don't always understand but you
Know all about us,
And now I'm reaching out to you,
Take my hand, as a father to his child.

Show you love me, Lord,
Lead me to a place of peace,
And show me the way ahead.
Don't let me down, Lord,
Because I am trusting you.

Alfred Shearing, *unemployed, of Brentwood, Essex.*

264 A prayer for a sick child

Lord Jesus Christ,

During your time on earth
  you blessed little children
  and laid your hands on the sick
  and restored them to health.
You are still mighty to heal and save.

I bring now into your presence
  this child [name] who is sick
I ask you, Lord, to lay your healing
  hands on him/her,
  give to him/her all that he/she needs
  for health of body, mind or spirit.

I ask you to bless the doctors and nurses
  and all who are caring for him/her
  guide them to a right judgement in all things
  and give them all the skill and patience
  which they need.

Thank you, Lord, for this hospital.
Bless all the hospital staff and all the
  children in their care at this time.
Bless also all other anxious parents,
  be with us, Lord, as we watch and wait.
May we each know your love, support and peace. Amen.

Revd Vincent Markland, *retired Anglican vicar and temporary hospital chaplain, of Swinton, Manchester.*

¡5 Idolatry

I cannot keep you for myself,
Nor hold you in the limits of my mind.
No system, book or liturgy
Contains your vast divinity.
I cannot hoard your love,
Or measure it in niceties.
To hold you here, or there,
You will not have.
My idols of the mind and sense
Have value that is all pretence.
Your Kingdom cannot be contained
In lifeless forms, or wooden words.
Grant, O Lord, that I may be
Free from such idolatry.

Emrys George, *retired Lloyd's underwriter, of Walthamstow, London E17.*

266 Haiku prayers for Pentecost

The author wrote these in the Japanese Haiku style after reading a book of Japanese poetry while in Cumbria, and recognising in it a form of verse suitable to Christian prayer.

Come, Holy Spirit,
Word of God in wind and fire,
Come, my heart inspire.

Come, Holy Spirit,
God in the evening breeze,
Come, my soul refresh.

Come, Holy Spirit,
Breath of God in us dwelling,
Come, in me abide.

Revd Peter Coppen, *retired Anglican vicar, of Greatworth, Banbury, Oxon.*

267 Remember

Perfect thoughts you can remember
Restoring solemnity
And honour to your life.
Yes, remember every word from the Lord,
Each blessing in divine Light.
Remember with me to please
His heavenly Heart. Amen.

Martine Pays, *of Streatham, south-west London.*

268 The Carnowen family prayer

This is a daily prayer used by four generations of a family brought up in rural Co. Monaghan, Ireland.

Thou God
Of all the families of the earth
We bless Thee for the ties of love
That bind our household together.
Bestow a very special blessing on everyone
Connected with our home – whether here or absent.
Thou knowest the needs of each of us –
Supply them out of Thy gracious fullness.

Let love and peace abound among us.

Bless the children.
May they learn of Jesus and follow him.
May they love one another and obey without murmuring.
May their words be always true
And their actions kind and good.

Bless those who serve.
May all of us be servants of Christ
Doing the will of God from the heart.

Grant to all our friends grace to walk patiently
In the path of righteousness
Rejoicing in the hope of the Gospel.

Gracious Father
Hear our prayer
For the sake of Jesus Christ
Thy Son.
Amen.

Kathleen Welsh (Lady Dunpark), *of Edinburgh, Scotland.*

269 During pain

So often, Lord in our pain, we are unable to hear Your voice.
Teach us to take time out of our busy situations to seek Your
guidance for our lives. Give us knowledge of Your love in the
quietness leading us to peace of mind for ourselves and those we
love. As we learn to trust You, from the pain can come strength.
Help us, then, to open up ourselves to the power of Your Holy
Spirit, to know that after the difficult times, joy and praise will
return. Because You have never ceased to love us, and never will
throughout our lives. You ask only for our trust and obedience so
that we will follow in the footsteps of Your beloved Son, Our Lord
Jesus Christ. Amen.

Mrs Cynthia Wixcey, *a housewife and church reader, of Cheltenham,
Gloucestershire.*

270 On walking in the mountain foothills

Dear Lord,
The beauty of Your world enfolds me
The crisp keen air
The water flowing, tumbling, murmuring
Colours grey, green – yellow gorse on the hill
Enduring rocks and fragile vegetation
White misty spray and pale blue sky above
The wonders of Your creation suffuse
        my mind with light
Fill me with a longing to be near You
To be enraptured in Your love and
To be held always and evermore in
Your Presence.

Mrs Kathleen Miller, *housewife, mother, grandmother, magistrate and
retired nurse, of East Morton, Keighley, West Yorkshire.*

271 A thank you for differences

*This prayer was written for use in the multi-faith assemblies at the
author's school.*

Dear Lord, thank you for our differences.
Thank you that although we are all different,
We can still be friends.
Help us to build up our friendship in you. Amen.

Margaret Inegbedion, *a part-time language support teacher, of
Bromham, Bedfordshire.*

272 No man has ever yet seen God (John 1:18)

O mystery most blessed, most holy
Most merciful, most loving, most mighty
Most true, most honourable, most beautiful
Unfathomable abyss of peace
Unutterable ocean of love
Fount of blessing
Giver of affection
Holy joy
Father, Son, Holy Ghost
One God in three persons
Ever to be worshipped and adored
Be thou to us
Rectitude, fortitude, beatitude
Refreshment, light, peace
Through Jesus Christ our Lord
Amen.

Revd Dr Harry Smythe, *former director of studies at Pusey House and of the Anglican Centre in Rome, retired in 1991 and now lives in Canterbury, Kent.*

273 Please God, help me to love my neighbour

Dear Lord, you told us to love our neighbours.
Please help me to express charity towards mine.
Please help me not to speak ill of them,
Nor discover their faults, however small or apparent.
Never let me show contempt,
Either in their presence,
Or in their absence.
Never let me repeat what has been said of them,
Nor be obstinate in my opinion,
Nor dispute or contest with heat,
Nor reprehend anyone over whom I have no authority.
Please help me to behave sweetly and charitably to everyone,
To harbour no aversion to my neighbours,
Neither to abstain from speaking to them,
Nor neglect to help them.
Never let me judge my neighbours.
Please help me to be charitable, Lord,
That we may all live in harmony.

Mrs Jan O'Leary, *a retired senior nurse, of Ely, Cambridgeshire.*

274 For Sundays

This is Your day, O Lord:
The day on which You rested after creating the world.
Help us in our observation of this day.
Where rest is possible for us,
May we rest in the confidence of Your love.
Where we have tasks,
May they be fulfilled to the best of our ability,
So that, however we use this day,
And whatever we achieve in it,
We may offer ourselves and all our actions
To You in faithful service. Amen.

Prudence Butler, *of Epsom, Surrey.*

275 A prayer for confidence

May we love life, and live a life of love.
May we breathe free, and feel the breath of God.
May we eat well in the Bread of Life.
May we raise our hopes, and hope indeed in God,
Believe in ourselves, and have blind faith in God,
Sing up, and sing in tune with God,
Speak up, and converse in truth with God.
May we listen long and hard.
Lord Jesus, You talk loud and clear.
Make me understand. Amen.

Genevieve Basto, *of north London.*

276 For the commuter

Dear Lord Jesus,
Keep us safe upon our travels.
Forgive our anger and frustration on the
busy highways. Give us patience when our
tempers fray, and give us understanding
for others in this busy life.

Let us be grateful for the means
to journey by sea and in the air, to
other lands and peoples.

Keep us in your protection always,
and bring us safely home. Amen.

Joyce Burt, *of Galmington, Taunton, Somerset.*

277 O God

O God, if there be a God, guide me
to know my duty. And if that duty
be hard, strengthen me to do it. Amen.

John Twells, *Darby Abbey, Derby.*

278 Before preaching a sermon

Father, open your word to us now; that we,
who need your grace so much, may not fail to
hear your voice, through Jesus Christ our Lord. Amen.

Arthur Circus, *semi-retired URC minister, of Great Wakering, Essex.*

279 Struggle

*The author gave up working in 1994 as a result of injury and since then
has written more than 250 prayers, of which this is the most recent.*

Sometimes, Lord, we struggle.
Don't know what to say to you,
We're too busy, restless,
Need to settle down, listen.

Well, I'm none the wiser,
Surrounded by books and thoughts,
Restlessness, want to be doing,
Not just sitting, waiting.

Start to read, become inspired,
Prayers of others always admired.
Quite often just left upon the shelf,
Instead of taking them to myself.

What riches in the pages,
Written down all the ages,
People who knew and loved you,
Wanted to share a word or two.

Thank you, Lord for your gift,
For minds, thoughts and inspiration,
For each new day you give,
Help our lives to be an offering.

Carol Pattinson, *of Milton Keynes.*

280 A prayer for the forgotten people

Let us pray for paper pushers
Let us appreciate administrators
Let us give heartfelt thanks for the nine-to-five people
Let us rejoice in those who risk the rat race.

Dear Lord, give them grace to do their jobs well
To complete with joy each task they have today.
Give them peace and friends and lead them to life.

Let us pray for drug pushers
Let us remember muggers
Let us give heartfelt thanks that Jesus came to save these people
Let us rejoice that there are Christians in the gutter
    who risk the rats and the cold.

Dear Lord, help us to take your love
    to the victims of sin and the sinners.
Give them peace and a family and lead them to life. Amen.

Mark Bennet, *of south-west London.*

Matthew Chi Ho Wong, aged 14

281 A prayer for those who work in hotels and restaurants

God our Father,
Whose Son Jesus Christ was born in a stable because
    there was no room in the inn,
Look with your favour on those who provide food
    and lodging on our roads and in our towns and cities;
Give them welcoming hearts and caring minds,
    that those whom they serve may be rested and refreshed;
Through Jesus Christ our Lord. Amen.

Canon Edward Noon, *of Wotton-under-Edge, Gloucestershire.*

282 Another day

Today's another day, Lord, the chance to start afresh:
    Yesterday I said this, Lord, and I know I made a mess...

I never greeted Mrs B, I was snappy on the phone,
    I was slapdash in my work, Lord, and I left poor S alone;

I could have given money to that tramp out on the hill,
I should have brought some flowers for my neighbour who is ill.

Thank You, Lord, for not despairing, and for listening to prayers,
    I humbly lay before You my troubles and my cares:

Each day there's hope I'll be, Lord, more loving in what I do,
    But I know I'll only manage by drawing close to You.

So daily take my hand, Lord, and as day creeps into night
May my 'candle flame' keep burning with a cheerful, glowing light.

Mrs Erica Burgon, *a retired PE teacher, of Cambridge.*

283 Christ on the Cross

This was written by a retired engineer and machine designer as an aid to Communion.

They stripped you bare and stole your clothes,
    and jeering passed you by;
They stretched you on a wooden cross
    and hung you out to die.

Now I before an altar stand,
    nor find a place of death
But with a living Lord contend,
    and my indwelling breath.

For you are my salvation, Lord,
   my hope and vision bright;
The all-revealing living word,
   and my indwelling light.

You are my indwelling Good,
   a presence all divine
Of God in human form bestowed,
   to be holy, to be mine.

So when I take you in my hand,
   my Lord, to life the key;
To all the world just bread and wine,
   to me your guarantee.

John Rae, *of Littlebourne, Canterbury, Kent.*

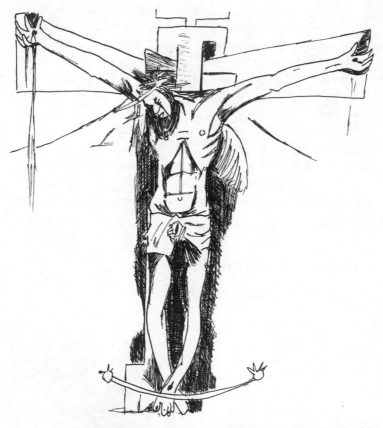

Derek Wing Hang Ho, aged 15

284 Prayer for those who are ill

The author regularly uses this prayer in his parish bulletin.

Lord Jesus, your hand cooled the fevered brow, strengthened the
weak limb and opened eye and ear to the beauty of your Father's
World. Be present to those dear to us, weakened by sickness and
whose strength to pray is burdened. Be at their side to carry their
cross, restore them to their families with deeper faith and stronger
body. Amen.

Fr Bernard Funnell, *parish priest of Our Lady and St Paul's,
Cleckheaton, in the Leeds diocese.*

285 Momentary prayer

Lord, I pray you'll hear me call,
Above the clamour from us all.
I am a moment in your time,
And you a moment, I confess, in mine.
Though my life is not that long,
Please, Lord, sweeten my life's song.

George Boileau, *of Toddington, Dunstable, Bedfordshire.*

286 A prayer to St Peter (feast day June 29)

*The author wrote this prayer to St Peter the Apostle because, as she says,
'I feel in many ways he is rather neglected – such a lovable man.'*

Salutations St Peter on this your feast day. I come to you in prayer
and with love and trust. Thank you for your humanity, for living
out the love that united you to Jesus; for the times when you
seemed to get things wrong; for your pains, your sorrows, your
joys as with the other apostles you spread the word of God.
Thank you for submitting to your cruel and painful death, for
accepting Jesus' invitation to follow him when you did not know
what he was asking of you. You were his chosen one. Through
you I praise and thank God for ordinary things.

There will be times when I will need to remember how Jesus
saved you from drowning when, heedless of the seas, you
plunged in and rushed to meet him. By your example may I learn
not to be afraid to plunge into whatever needs to be done,
trusting to God that he will give me the help I need.

When I make mistakes or turn away from those who need my help and when I deny God's love and power and justice, not three times but thirty-three, pray for me and stay close so that I may learn not to be overwhelmed by my weaknesses but to accept them for what they are and with God's blessing continue on my way. Pray for me, St Peter, that my prayer becomes a reality and the centre of my life.

Thanks and praise to God, the beginning and the end.

Joan Baker, *of Chathill, Northumberland.*

287 A judge's plea

The author has used this prayer in intercession at his local church, Holy Trinity at Amberley.

O Lord, we mourn today the passing of those we love, but we do not mourn the passing of the years, for the years are yours. We thank you for all that makes them rich and rewarding – for good health, for energy and intelligence, for friendship and love, and for the priceless gift of laughter. Help us, O Lord, sometimes to laugh at ourselves, and help us, too, in your name, to fight the evils of the world – poverty, prejudice, lies and hatred. Help us every day to preach a sermon – not with our lips but with our lives. And help us to remember when things go wrong, and our burdens seem too heavy to bear, that your loving-kindness, your compassion and your mercy, are with us always. Rejoicing in the fellowship of all your saints, we commend ourselves and all Christian people to your unfailing love.

His Honour Peter Mason, *a retired senior circuit judge, of Amberley, near Stroud, Gloucestershire.*

288 At last

How wondrous it will be, Dear Lord,
When I am called to rest.
To leave behind all earthly cares
And by thyself be blessed.
Now I have had a happy life,
Much joy on earth I've known.
A loving husband, lots of friends,
A baby of mine own.
But I shall need some tender arms
To guide me on my way.
To help me should I stumble,
Please teach me how to pray.
What wonderful reunions
With loved ones there will be.
And shall I have the privilege
Of thy dear face to see?

Mrs Nancy Williams, *a housewife, of Highcliffe-on-Sea, Christchurch, Dorset.*

William Haynes, aged 16

188 Morning prayer

A restful sleep the long night ends
New dawn – on God my strength depends.
Of all my faculties aware,
On thee dear Lord I cast my care.
My I find joy and willing zest,
To serve thee Lord as thou knows best.

When noon day sun with golden beam
Sheds out its rays, my soul redeem,
Give me a listening ear to care,
My neighbour's trouble may I share.
Untimely deeds thy truth to prove
In witness of thine endless love.

Thy grace and comfort be my guide,
A quiet hymn at eventide.
My grateful prayer to thee ascends.
As restful peace on me descends.
For ever in thy footsteps we
Must follow – bring us nearer thee.

Beatrice Johnson, *retired district nurse, of Wigan, Lancashire.*